STONEWALL KITCHEN

APPETIZERS

STONEWALL KITCHEN
APPETIZERS
Finger Foods and Small Plates

BY JONATHAN KING, JIM STOTT & KATHY GUNST

Photographs by Jim Stott

CHRONICLE BOOKS

SAN FRANCISCO

Text copyright © 2010 by Jonathan King, Jim Stott, and Kathy Gunst.
Photographs copyright © 2010 by Jim Stott.

Library of Congress Cataloging-in-Publication Data available.

ISBN 978-0-8118-6869-3

Manufactured in China.

Designed by Katie Heit
Prop styling by Andrea Kuhn
Food styling by Catrine Kelty

10 9 8 7 6 5 4 3 2 1

Chronicle Books LLC
680 Second Street
San Francisco, California 94107
www.chroniclebooks.com

DEDICATION

To our family and friends and the wonderful guests of Stonewall Kitchen
who have supported us from our beginnings—even in the rain at the
local farmers' market.
—J.K. and J. S.

To John, Maya, and Emma
—K.G.

ACKNOWLEDGMENTS

We were lucky to have an amazing team working on this book. Many thanks to
Catrine Kelty, our food stylist who made all these delicious appetizers look so gorgeous;
Andrea Kuhn, prop stylist, for her impeccable taste; John McNeil, assistant photographer,
for his great eye; and Kim Gallagher, assistant food stylist, for all her help.

We are grateful to Amy Treadwell, our editor and visionary, and to Peter Perez for
his marketing genius. Thanks to our agent, Doe Coover, for schlepping up to Maine
over and over again and helping us make the books we always wanted to make.

TABLE OF CONTENTS

CHAPTER 3
Small Plates

INTRODUCTION

What makes appetizers so appealing? While everyone looks forward to the main course, the appetizers are frequently the stars of the meal. Nothing matches the simple appeal and deep satisfaction of having a small plate of delicious food set in front of you. Appetizers offer an opportunity to enjoy new flavors and textures that you might not consider for the meal's centerpiece. Pop one into your mouth and experience a burst of flavor that wakes up your taste buds, or take a spoonful and enjoy a soothing experience that helps you settle in for the rest of the meal.

We often find ourselves gazing at restaurant menus and ordering three or four appetizers instead of a main course. Appetizers make us feel like kids in a candy store—looking at all those goodies and realizing that we can have not just one, or even two, but maybe three or four. Appetizers tend to be our favorite foods. So we thought: Why not devote an entire book to the world's best appetizers?

This book celebrates the art of the small plate (or bowl).

We offer appetizer recipes from around the world—the best of many diverse cuisines. Some of the most interesting food in the world focuses on small portions. For example, tapas—the traditional small plates that are served in bars and restaurants throughout Spain—have become hugely popular in the United States. These savory bites of marinated olives, cheeses, spicy sausages, roasted peppers, and creamy croquettes inspire us. There are also the famed *meze* platters of the Middle East and Mediterranean—the fabulous plates and bowls of olives and hummus and eggplant spreads, plus squares of creamy spinach and feta pie. There is the antipasto of Italy, offering cheeses, salamis, breadsticks, olives, pickled vegetables, and more. The *amuse-bouche* of France is a chef's way of tickling the palate before dinner, literally to "entertain the mouth" for the meal to come.

We've combed our culinary memories, from travels both near and far, to bring you the best appetizers. From the Middle East, we offer Lamb and Feta Sliders (page 147), which are really just fabulous meatballs served on tiny pita crackers; silky hummus (page 29); Eggplant "Caviar" with Tomato-Mint Salad (page 114); crispy Pita Crackers (page 73); and Middle Eastern–style Meatballs with Spiced Yogurt-Mint Sauce (page 89). From Spain, we have a Potato and Scallion Tortilla (page 96)—a delicious frittata-like egg dish; Chickpeas and Chorizo (page 93); Littleneck Clams in Green Garlic Sauce (page 81); and Spanish-Style Empanadas (page 59). There are Asian Pork and

Shrimp Dumplings with Chile-Cilantro-Soy Dipping Sauce (page 85); Italian Pumpkin Ravioli with Brown Butter and Sage (page 82); Scandinavian Gravlax with Mustard-Dill Sauce (page 117); Mexican-style Crab Tostadas with Avocado and Lime-Cilantro Cream (page 121); French Chicken Liver Pâté (page 64); buttery, spiced Cheese Twists with Parmesan, Rosemary, and Cayenne (page 35); and Indian-Spiced Cauliflower Soup with Spiced Cashews (page 78).

But we didn't forget those recipes closer to home that we love. We gave a new twist to a few American classics, including a Five-Onion Dip (page 20), a savory whirl of five kinds of onions cooked slowly until they caramelize. It's a fresh, satisfying nod to the packaged onion soup dip we all grew up with. There's Mini Mac and Cheese (page 129), baked in a mini muffin tray, and Cheese Balls Redux (page 50)—those mainstays of 1950s cocktail parties—that are *so* ready to be back in style again. We have reinvented them with blue cheese, dates, and pancetta, all dusted with toasted walnuts. We even reinvented popcorn (page 30) and spiced nuts (page 33) by mixing them with fabulous spices and flavorings.

You'll find this book set up a bit differently than most. We've divided *Stonewall Kitchen Appetizers* into first courses we eat with our fingers ("Finger Food"), those that are best served in a bowl ("Small Bowls"), and the dishes that are best eaten with a fork and knife ("Small Plates").

We also offer a few of our favorite cocktail recipes, some ideas for appetizer party menus, tips for how much to serve, and innovative presentation ideas for family dinners or parties. And we have been really conscious of providing recipes that can be made well ahead of time (and assembled just before serving), making this collection ideal for entertaining.

We've had a great time throwing some appetizer-only parties. We mix up a few of our favorite cocktails, choose four or five appetizers, and make a meal of it. Think about throwing a Spanish-style tapas party (see page 153), a Middle Eastern–themed party (see page 149), or an Italian antipasti party (see page 150). No one will even ask about a main course. The truth is that the appetizers are always the most creative part of the meal anyway. So here's to having the first course be the most memorable.

Enjoy!

—Jonathan King, Jim Stott, and Kathy Gunst

THROWING A COCKTAIL/APPETIZER PARTY: THE FACTS

Cocktail parties sound like such a great, carefree idea. You buy some good wine, maybe some Champagne, mix a few cocktails, and put together some party food. But when you get down to actually cooking and making the lists, it can be overwhelming. The recipes in this book are designed to make entertaining— whether it's for your family or a huge cocktail party— easy and satisfying.

Here are a few basics for throwing an appetizer or a cocktail party:

* As with any party, do as much ahead as possible. Get out napkins, serving platters, serving spoons, ice buckets, martini shakers, etc. Think ahead about what you'll need and get everything ready so you don't stress out looking for something at the last minute.

* Choose a menu that balances do-ahead dishes with ones that require last-minute details. You also want to offer hot foods as well as cold options. Always have several simple cold foods, such as olives, dips, cheeses, pâtés, and smoked fish, ready when people arrive, and then bring out the more complex hot foods at intervals throughout the party.

* When planning a cocktail party and trying to determine how much food to serve, there are several factors to consider. If the party consists of cocktails and appetizers *to be followed by dinner,* you only need to serve 2 to 3 different appetizers. To

determine how much food to make, figure 3 to 5 bites per person for each appetizer you serve.

* If you are planning an appetizer-only party (no dinner), you should figure on serving between 4 and 12 dishes. For example, if you're having 20 people, you might want to offer 6 dishes of 3 to 5 bites per person. If it's a larger gathering, offer 10 to 12 different appetizers with 3 to 4 bites per person. It's best to have too much (leftovers can always be frozen).

* Have a number of dishes that appeal to vegetarians.

* Another factor to consider is the length of the party.

You want to stagger the food over several hours so that everything isn't placed out for guests during the beginning of the party—which inevitably means you run out of food by the end of the party when people have been drinking for a while.

* You can really get creative and fun with food presentation at cocktail parties. Think about adding an interesting visual element to the plate underneath the food. For instance, with oysters or seafood, a bed of kosher or sea salt lining the plate adds an eye-catching detail. Think about lining plates with black or white beans (and placing the food on top), or foods that use citrus can be placed on top of thin slices of lemons, limes, or oranges. Serve savory dishes atop sprigs of fresh herbs and edible flowers. These form a bed for the foods and add great color and texture to the plate.

* Serve soup in shot glasses or tiny espresso cups (so everyone has a taste without filling up). Serve seafood and small bites in oversized Asian soup-

spoons (which tend to be very inexpensive and are available at many Asian food markets and specialty food stores). Serve appetizers on tiered trays, cake plates, or mirrors.

* Think about how you want to present the food. Do you want a buffet or do you want to pass hors d'oeuvres? Professional caterers talk about "stations" at a party. Do you want one station where all the food will be offered on one table? Or do you want to serve a big platter of cheese, olives, fruit, and crackers at one station and then have another station for raw seafood and another for hot appetizers? The more stations you offer, the more the party can flow from space to space as people move around the room tasting a bit of everything. A "station" can simply mean using different sides of a room or using several tables. Keep it simple!

* When serving higher-end foods like caviar, oysters, and shrimp, you may want to pass those on a tray so you can control how much everyone eats. If you leave a tray of shrimp on a table, people tend to take a whole lot more than if you pass the tray and offer them one or two. You also need to consider how long perishable foods will be out of refrigeration, so passing trays helps control that.

Check out the menus on page 149 for specific party ideas and themes.

1

CHAPTER

FINGER FOOD

ORANGE AND CHILE–SPICED OLIVES

MAKES 1½ CUPS

Look for good-quality kalamata or oil-cured olives or use a brine-cured green olive. We love to make up a big batch of these olives and snack on them all week or serve them with cocktails or as part of an antipasto platter. Experiment with flavors; see our variation ideas.

INGREDIENTS

1½ cups olives (see headnote), drained

Juice and zest of 1 large or 2 small oranges

⅓ cup olive oil

1 clove garlic, very thinly sliced (optional)

About ⅛ teaspoon crushed red pepper flakes or chile pepper

In a medium bowl, mix the olives with the remaining ingredients. Taste the mixture and see if you want to add a touch more red pepper flakes for spicier olives. Let marinate for about an hour at room temperature. Transfer the olives to a jar and cover and refrigerate. The olives will keep for several days.

VARIATIONS:

Add lemon juice and lemon zest instead of orange.

Add 1½ teaspoons fennel or cumin seeds, lightly crushed.

Add 1 tablespoon finely chopped fresh herbs such as rosemary, thyme, basil, oregano, or lemon verbena.

FIVE-ONION DIP

MAKES ABOUT 2½ CUPS

Remember that great dip of your childhood? You sprinkled the dry packet of dehydrated onions into a bowl of sour cream and dipped salty potato chips in and, well, it was pure comfort food. Our version is made with five members of the onion family—red, sweet Vidalia, shallots, leeks, and garlic—cooked long and slow so their natural sugars emerge. The caramelized onions are then deglazed with balsamic vinegar and mixed up with sour cream. The result? That same delicious creamy dip—with pure onion flavors and no additives. Serve the dip with potato chips, Pita Crackers (page 73), or raw vegetables.

INGREDIENTS

3 tablespoons olive oil	2 shallots (about 4 ounces), very thinly sliced
2 medium red onions (about 10 ounces), very thinly sliced	2 cloves garlic, thinly sliced
1 large Vidalia onion (about 8 ounces), very thinly sliced	Salt
	Freshly ground black pepper
	½ cup balsamic vinegar
1 leek (about 6 ounces), cut lengthwise and thinly sliced	1¼ cups sour cream
	Hot pepper sauce

1. Heat the oil in a very large skillet over low heat. Add the onions, leek, shallots, garlic, and salt and pepper to taste. Cook, stirring occasionally, for about 45 minutes. The onions are ready when they are soft, golden, and sweet. Add the vinegar and cook for another 15 minutes, stirring frequently, until the mixture is golden brown. Remove from the heat and let cool slightly.

2. In the container of a food processor, puree the onion mixture with the sour cream until somewhat thick and chunky. Remove to a bowl and taste for seasoning; add salt, pepper, and hot pepper sauce to taste.

RED CAVIAR AND MEYER LEMON DIP

MAKES ABOUT 1½ CUPS

You don't need to sell your grandmother's jewelry to make this delicious, colorful dip; red caviar—the roe (eggs) of salmon—is relatively inexpensive and easy to find. We mix it into this simple dip with scallions, sour cream, fresh chives, and sweet Meyer lemon juice. If you can't find Meyer lemons (available during the winter months), you can easily substitute regular lemon juice.

Serve with Pita Crackers (page 73), potato chips, endive spears, thin slices of cucumber, raw vegetables, or small pieces of thin black bread.

INGREDIENTS

1½ cups sour cream

2 scallions, minced
(white and green parts)

½ teaspoon grated
Meyer lemon zest

1½ tablespoons freshly
squeezed Meyer lemon juice

1½ tablespoons chopped
fresh chives

½ cup red salmon
or other caviar

Freshly ground black pepper

1. In a medium bowl, mix together the sour cream, scallions, lemon zest, lemon juice, and 1 tablespoon of the chives. Gently fold in half the caviar. Season with pepper. The dip can be covered and refrigerated for up to 24 hours.

2. To serve, spoon the remaining caviar on top of the dip and sprinkle with the remaining chives.

VARIATION:
Spread 1 teaspoon of the dip on a thin slice of English cucumber and garnish with a tiny sprig of fresh chervil or dill. Serve on an oversized spoon.

SMOKED SALMON AND CAPER SPREAD

MAKES ABOUT 1 CUP

This is the kind of spread or dip you can whip together in about five minutes. We whirl smoked salmon, cream cheese, and capers in a food processor to make an instant spread for thinly sliced brown bread, bagel chips, crackers, vegetables, or cooked shrimp.

INGREDIENTS

8 ounces smoked salmon

1 cup cream cheese, at room temperature

3½ tablespoons capers, drained

Freshly ground black pepper

Place all the ingredients, including the pepper to taste, in the container of a food processor and blend until almost smooth. Place the spread in a crock or ramekin, smooth the top, and serve. You can make the spread 24 hours ahead of time; cover and refrigerate until needed.

VARIATIONS:

Add 1 teaspoon grated lemon zest.

Add 1 tablespoon chopped fresh chives to the dip and sprinkle about 1 teaspoon chopped fresh chives on top.

Substitute smoked trout or any smoked fish for the salmon.

Add a few tablespoons of red salmon caviar to the top of the dip for an extravagant garnish.

Sprinkle the top of the spread with assorted microgreens.

COCKTAILS, ANYONE?

Appetizers and cocktails are good friends. They go together like Fred and Ginger—natural partners. Here we offer a favorite from each one of us. Make up a pitcher of each of these three cocktails, choose four or five of your favorite recipes from the book, and invite over a small crowd of your favorite people. Sounds like a party!

Jim's Favorite: The Bellini
SERVES 4 TO 8
2 very ripe peaches, peeled, pitted, and diced
1 tablespoon freshly squeezed lemon juice
1 teaspoon sugar
One 750-milliliter bottle Prosecco sparkling wine, chilled

Put the peaches, lemon juice, and sugar in the bowl of a food processor and process until smooth. Press the mixture through a fine-mesh sieve and discard the peach solids in the sieve. Put 2 tablespoons of the peach puree into each Champagne glass and fill with cold Prosecco. Serve immediately.

Jonathan's Favorite: Dark & Stormy
SERVES 1
Ice cubes
2 lime wedges
2 ounces dark rum
10 ounces ginger beer

Fill a 12-ounce glass with ice. Squeeze 1 lime wedge over the ice and drop into the glass. Pour the rum into the glass, then add the ginger beer. Stir lightly and garnish with the second lime wedge.

Kathy's Favorite: Negroni
SERVES 1
2 ounces vodka
1 ounce Campari
1 ounce sweet vermouth
Ice cubes
1 spiral orange zest

Pour the vodka, Campari, and vermouth into a cocktail shaker with several cubes of ice. Shake until mixed and well chilled and strain into a martini glass. Place the spiral of orange zest on the rim of the glass and serve.

CHUNKY GUACAMOLE

SERVES 4 TO 6

We love the fresh flavors and textures in this guacamole. Unlike so many versions of the classic Mexican dip, ours isn't mashed or mushy, but features cubes of fresh avocado, crunchy green bell pepper, juicy tomatoes, spicy jalapeño, earthy cilantro, and fresh lime juice. You can serve it in a bowl, but it's extra special if you fill a 2-inch biscuit cutter with the guacamole and then remove the cutter for a perfectly rounded individual serving. Top with fresh cilantro leaves and serve with tortilla chips.

INGREDIENTS

2 ripe avocados, not mushy but ripe, flesh cut into ½-inch cubes

6 ounces cherry tomatoes or heirloom tomatoes, chopped

1 small (sweet) green bell pepper, finely chopped

2 scallions, finely chopped (white and green parts)

¼ cup minced fresh cilantro, plus fresh cilantro sprigs for garnish

About ½ jalapeño pepper, minced (see Note)

2½ tablespoons olive oil

Juice of 1 large lime

Salt

Freshly ground black pepper

Hot pepper sauce

In a medium bowl, gently mix together the avocados, tomatoes, bell pepper, scallions, minced cilantro, jalapeño to taste, oil, and lime juice. Add salt, pepper, and hot pepper sauce to taste. Serve cold or at room temperature, garnished with the cilantro sprigs.

NOTE:

If you want a guacamole with a really spicy bite, add almost the entire pepper with the seeds. If you want just a bit of fire, add half with the seeds. If you prefer a mild guacamole, add the entire minced pepper without any of the seeds.

MIDDLE EASTERN HUMMUS

Creamy and rich with chickpeas, tahini (sesame paste), lemon juice, garlic, and olive oil, this dip can be made in just about ten minutes. We like to surround the dip with cumin- and cayenne-scented Indian-Spiced Cashews. Serve with Pita Crackers (page 73) and an assortment of good olives. The Eggplant "Caviar" with Tomato-Mint Salad (page 114) is also delicious served with this hummus.

INGREDIENTS

One 20-ounce can chickpeas, drained, rinsed in cold water, and drained again

¼ cup tahini (sesame paste)

¼ cup olive oil

3 tablespoons freshly squeezed lemon juice

1 large or 2 small cloves garlic, chopped

Dash of ground cumin

Dash of cayenne pepper, plus some for garnish

Salt

Freshly ground black pepper

¾ to 1 cup Indian-Spiced Cashews (page 33), coarsely chopped

1. In the container of a food processor or blender, combine the chickpeas, tahini, oil, ¼ cup water, the lemon juice, garlic, cumin, cayenne, and salt and pepper to taste. Blend until smooth. The texture should be thick but creamy. Add more water if needed; season to taste with the cumin, cayenne, salt, and pepper. Place the hummus in a low, wide serving bowl.

2. Surround the hummus with a thin circle of the chopped spiced nuts. Sprinkle a very light dusting of cayenne in the center.

POPCORN: THREE VARIATIONS ON A THEME

MAKES ABOUT 6 CUPS; SERVES 6 TO 8

Popcorn as an appetizer? Sure! It's all the rage served with sophisticated cocktails at chic bars around the country—bowls of popcorn flavored with everything from truffle oil to Indian spices to garlic and cheese. Try any of these flavor combinations and then have fun playing with flavors to think up your own variety.

INGREDIENTS

1½ tablespoons canola oil

½ cup white or yellow popcorn kernels

Prepared flavor toppings (following)

Sea salt or garlic salt

Freshly ground black pepper

1. In a large pot, heat the oil over low heat for 3 to 4 minutes. Add the popcorn kernels in a single layer on the bottom of the pot, stir well, and cover. Cook until the corn starts popping. Once the corn is popping, shake the pan back and forth so that the kernels are evenly distributed. Cook until the kernels stop popping.

2. Remove the popcorn from the pot and place in a large bowl. Toss in your preferred flavoring while the popcorn is still hot and put the lid from the pot over the bowl; toss well to incorporate the flavoring throughout all the popcorn. Season with salt and pepper. Serve immediately.

FLAVOR TOPPINGS

White Truffle: ½ to 1 tablespoon white truffle oil and 1 tablespoon olive oil.

Cheese, Thyme, and Pepper: ¼ to ⅓ cup grated Parmesan (or your favorite hard) cheese, 1½ teaspoons dried thyme (or 1 tablespoon fresh, chopped), and extra black pepper to taste.

Spicy Turmeric Butter and Cheddar: Melt 4 tablespoons butter with ¼ teaspoon cayenne, ¼ teaspoon mild chili powder, and 1 teaspoon ground turmeric. Cook, stirring, until the butter turns a gorgeous yellow and has a spicy flavor. Add ½ packed cup finely grated sharp Cheddar cheese when ready to toss.

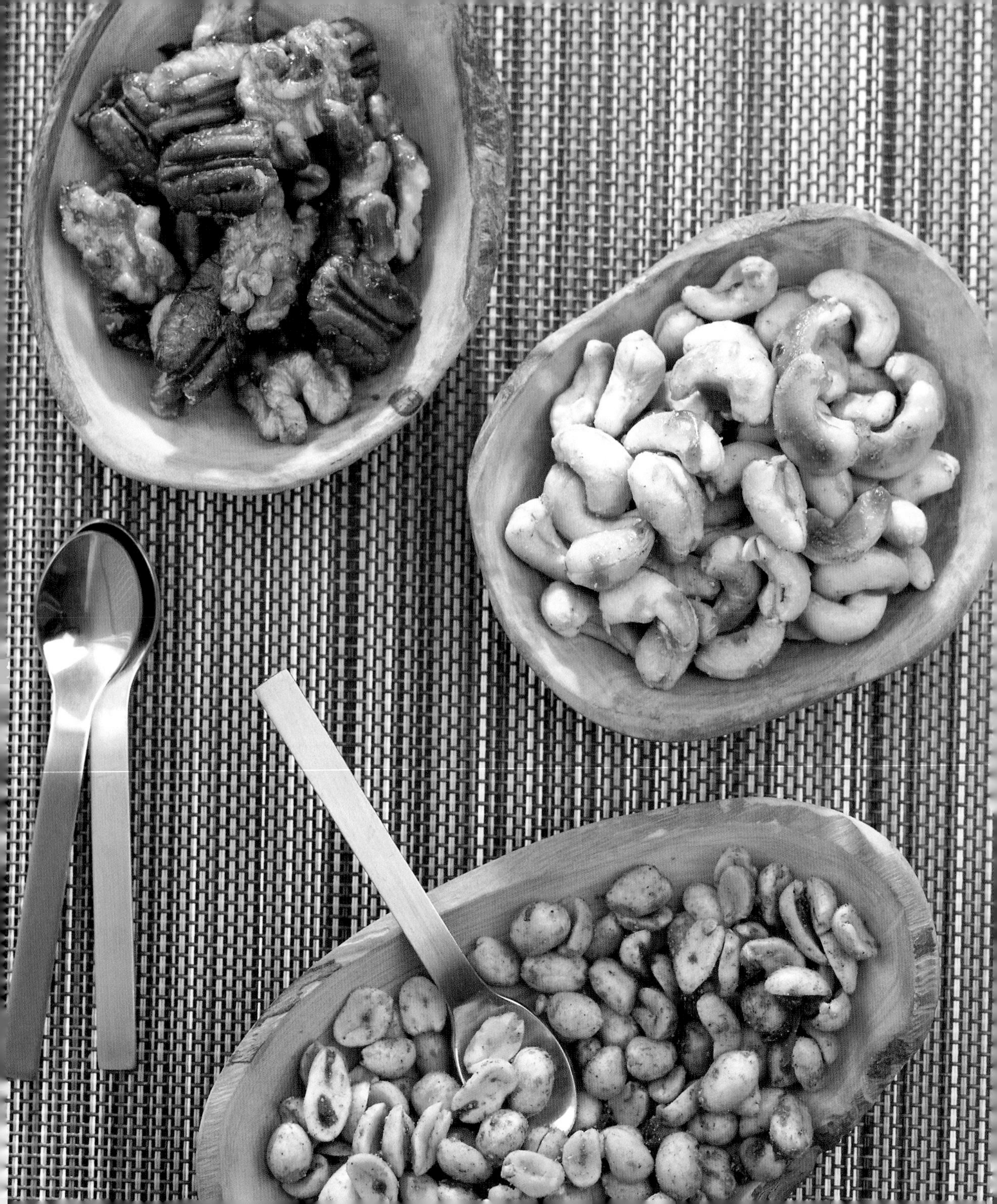

SPICED NUTS:
THREE VARIATIONS ON A THEME

Feel free to substitute or add nuts other than the ones specified in each recipe. The spiced nuts will keep for two to three days in a well-sealed jar in a dark, cool spot.

INDIAN-SPICED CASHEWS

MAKES 1 CUP

Hot, sweet, and flavored with exotic spices, we like to serve these nuts with salads, curries, or simply a cold beer or dry martini.

INGREDIENTS
1 teaspoon olive oil
1 teaspoon butter
¼ teaspoon ground cumin
¼ teaspoon ground turmeric
¼ teaspoon hot curry powder
Dash of cayenne pepper
Salt
Freshly ground black pepper
1 cup (5 ounces) lightly salted cashews
2 tablespoons honey

1. In a medium skillet, heat the oil and butter over low heat. Add the cumin, turmeric, curry, cayenne, and salt and pepper to taste. Cook, stirring the spices into the oil, for about 30 seconds. Add the cashews and stir well, making sure to coat all the nuts with the spices; cook for 2 minutes. Add the honey and stir well to coat all the nuts; cook for 2 minutes more, until the nuts are golden brown and well glazed.

2. Pour the nuts onto a sheet of parchment paper or aluminum foil, spreading them out so they don't clump together. Let cool and remove from the paper.

SPICED MIXED NUTS

MAKES 1½ CUPS

These nuts are equally good served with cocktails or sprinkled over salads, soups, and stews.

INGREDIENTS
2 tablespoons olive oil
½ teaspoon ground ginger
½ teaspoon curry powder
¼ teaspoon cayenne pepper
2 tablespoons sugar
1 tablespoon honey or maple syrup
1 cup (5 ounces) pecan halves
½ cup (2½ ounces) walnut halves
Salt (optional)

Continued...

... continued

1. Line a baking sheet with waxed or parchment paper. Lightly oil the paper.

2. Heat the oil in a large skillet over medium heat. Add the ginger, curry, and cayenne and cook, stirring, for about 15 seconds. Stir in the sugar and honey and mix well. Add the pecans and walnuts and stir to completely coat the nuts; cook for about 5 minutes, stirring occasionally, until the nuts are caramelized and have turned a pale golden brown.

3. Pour the nuts onto the prepared baking sheet, spreading them out so they don't clump together. Let cool and sprinkle lightly with salt, if desired.

ASIAN-SPICED PEANUTS

MAKES 1 CUP

Plain old peanuts take on a fiery, exotic flavor when they're tossed with crushed red chile pepper and Chinese five-spice powder—a blend of cinnamon, cloves, fennel, star anise, and Szechwan peppercorns that is available in Asian markets and many supermarkets.

INGREDIENTS

2 teaspoons butter

1 small dried red chile pepper, minced, with or without seeds (see Note)

1 teaspoon Chinese five-spice powder

½ teaspoon ground ginger

1 cup (5 ounces) roasted, unsalted peanuts

Salt

Freshly ground black pepper

1. Melt the butter in a medium skillet over low heat. Add the chile and cook for 10 seconds, stirring. Add the five-spice powder and ginger and cook, stirring, for another 10 seconds or so, until the spices are well incorporated into the butter. Add the peanuts, and salt and pepper to taste and cook, stirring, for 2 minutes, until the nuts are well coated with spices and beginning to turn golden brown.

2. Pour the nuts onto a piece of parchment paper or aluminum foil to cool. Serve at room temperature.

NOTE:
Add the chile pepper seeds if you want a peanut with a real bite.

CHEESE TWISTS WITH PARMESAN, ROSEMARY, AND CAYENNE

MAKES 24 TWISTS

This is exactly what you're looking for when you want something simple but elegant to serve at your next cocktail party. We season puff pastry with olive oil, grated Parmesan cheese, earthy rosemary, and a touch of fiery cayenne to make full-flavored cheese straws. These taste like those fancy, expensive ones you see in French bakeries and—trust us—they are every bit as good. The secret? We use premade puff pastry (we always keep a box in the freezer) that allows us to make these cheese twists in less than thirty minutes—from start to finish. They can be made several days ahead of time; cover in an airtight container and store in a cool, dark spot. The buttery dough and spices make these twists hard to resist; best to make a double batch and freeze some for a rainy day!

INGREDIENTS

2 sheets puff pastry (1 pound), thawed if frozen, but well chilled

About ⅓ cup olive oil

Salt (see Note)

Freshly ground black pepper

About 1 cup grated Parmesan cheese

¼ cup finely chopped fresh rosemary

Cayenne pepper

1. Place a rack in the middle of the oven and preheat to 400 degrees F.

2. Lay the pastry sheets on a clean work surface. Spread each sheet lightly with some of the oil, rubbing it all over the dough with your fingers. Sprinkle each sheet with salt and pepper, ¼ cup of the Parmesan, 1 tablespoon of the rosemary, and a light sprinkling of cayenne. Use your hands to lightly press the ingredients into the dough. Gently flip the pastry over and repeat with the Parmesan, rosemary, and cayenne.

3. Use a pizza cutter to cut each sheet lengthwise into ½- to ¾-inch strips. You should have a total of 24 strips. Hold a strip of dough at each end and twist

Continued …

…continued

the dough to create a spiral. Place it on an ungreased baking sheet, lightly pressing the ends to keep them from unrolling. Repeat with the remaining strips, dividing them between 2 baking sheets and making sure not to let the pastries touch each other.

4. Bake for 6 minutes. Very gently flip the twists over and bake for another 6 minutes, or until they are a pale golden brown on both sides. Remove and serve warm or at room temperature.

NOTE:

Only use a dash of salt since the Parmesan cheese can be quite salty.

VARIATIONS:

Use sharp Cheddar cheese instead of the Parmesan.

Use fresh thyme, oregano, basil, and/or chives instead of the rosemary.

Use an herb-flavored olive oil instead of plain olive oil.

Add ½ teaspoon each of curry powder, ground cumin, and dried oregano instead of the rosemary for a Middle Eastern–flavored twist.

Add a sprinkling of sesame or poppy seeds to the dough, pressing the seeds into the pastry lightly to make sure they adhere.

Add a touch of grated lemon or orange zest.

WHITE BEAN CROSTINI WITH OLIVE AND SUN-DRIED TOMATO TOPPING

SERVES 3 TO 4

We love transforming canned white beans into a silky smooth, flavorful dip in just a matter of minutes. Simply sauté garlic in olive oil, add the beans and scallions, and puree. We toast good crusty bread and spread the white bean mixture on top and then add black olives and sun-dried tomatoes. You can also serve the white beans as a dip surrounded by the olive and sun-dried tomato mixture and accompanied with Pita Crackers (page 73), toast, or chips and lots of crudités.

INGREDIENTS

2½ tablespoons olive oil

1 teaspoon Basil Oil (page 109; optional)

1 clove garlic, chopped

2 scallions, chopped (white and green parts)

One 15-ounce can white beans, drained, rinsed, and drained again

1½ tablespoons chopped fresh rosemary

1½ tablespoons freshly squeezed lemon juice

Salt

Freshly ground black pepper

¼ cup coarsely chopped pitted black olives

¼ cup coarsely chopped oil-packed sun-dried tomatoes, with the oil

Six ½-inch slices ciabatta or crusty bread

Microgreens for garnish (optional)

1. In a large skillet, heat 1 tablespoon of the olive oil and the basil oil (if using) over low heat. Add the garlic and cook for 1 minute. Add the scallions and cook for 2 minutes, stirring. Add the beans, rosemary, lemon juice, and salt and pepper to taste. Stir and cook for 3 minutes, until well incorporated. Transfer the mixture to the container of a food processor. Blend until

Continued...

…*continued*

almost smooth. Remove and taste for seasoning. (The bean puree can be made 24 hours ahead of time; cover and refrigerate.)

2. In a small bowl, mix together the olives and sun-dried tomatoes with any of the oil from the tomatoes and set aside; cover and refrigerate until ready to use.

3. Preheat the broiler. Place the bread slices on a baking sheet. Using a pastry brush or the back of a spoon, drizzle half of the remaining olive oil on top and broil them for 1 to 2 minutes, or until a pale golden brown. Flip the toasts over and drizzle the remaining oil on top. Broil for 1 minute more, until pale golden brown. Remove from the broiler. (The toasts can be made several hours ahead of time. Once they have cooled completely, keep in a cool, dark spot in a tightly sealed plastic bag.)

4. Spread a heaping tablespoon of the bean puree on each piece of toast. Spoon 1 tablespoon of the olive-tomato mixture in the center. Serve at room temperature. You can serve the toasts whole or cut in half for smaller, bite-size portions. Top with microgreens, if you like.

ROASTED GARLIC BRUSCHETTA WITH STEAK TIPS

SERVES 3 TO 4

When you want to serve something elegant that can mostly be made ahead of time, this is the dish you are looking for. We roast a whole head of garlic and mash the soft cloves with olive oil. Toasted slices of crusty ciabatta or French bread are spread with the roasted garlic and then topped with thin slices of grilled or sautéed steak tips. There are a variety of additional toppings you can choose from. This recipe can easily be doubled or tripled to feed a crowd.

INGREDIENTS

1 head garlic, ¼ inch cut off the top to just expose the cloves

¼ cup olive oil

Salt

Freshly ground black pepper

Eight ½-inch slices crusty ciabatta, French bread, or Italian bread

12 ounces steak tips or flatiron steak, cut into 1½-inch strips

3 tablespoons finely chopped fresh parsley

1. Place a rack in the middle of the oven and preheat to 350 degrees F.

2. Place the garlic in a small ovenproof skillet or gratin dish and pour 1 tablespoon of the oil over the top of the garlic onto the exposed cloves. Season lightly with salt and pepper. Roast the garlic for 40 to 50 minutes, or until the cloves feel soft when you squeeze them or test them with a small, sharp knife. Remove the garlic from the oven and let it cool for just a few minutes.

3. Once the garlic is cool enough to handle without burning yourself, squeeze the cloves from the skins into a bowl (discard the skins). Sprinkle lightly with salt and, using a regular kitchen fork, mash the garlic into a thick paste. Add 2 tablespoons of the remaining oil to the puree and season with pepper. The garlic puree can be made 1 hour ahead of time. Cover and keep in a cool, dark spot; it need not be refrigerated.

Continued…

...continued

4. Preheat the broiler. Place the bread slices on a baking sheet. Broil them for 1 to 2 minutes, or just until the bread begins to turn a golden brown. Do not let it burn. Remove from the oven and flip the bread over. Divide the garlic puree between the toasts and spread it evenly on each slice. Broil for another 1 to 2 minutes, or until the toasts just begin to brown. Remove from the oven. The toasts can be made several hours ahead of time; cover loosely and keep in a cool, dark spot; they need not be refrigerated.

5. Just before serving, heat a large skillet over high heat with the remaining 1 tablespoon oil. Add the steak tips, sprinkle with salt and pepper, and cook, undisturbed, for 4 minutes. Carefully flip the meat over, season again, and cook for another 4 to 5 minutes, until the meat is well browned and medium-rare inside. Alternately, you can cook the beef on a hot gas or charcoal grill on a grill tray for 4 to 5 minutes per side. Remove from the heat and let the meat sit for 1 minute. Thinly slice the meat on the diagonal. Place 2 to 3 thin slices of beef on top of each piece of garlic bread and sprinkle lightly with parsley.

VARIATIONS:
You can add any of the following toppings to the beef:

Thinly sliced jarred sweet pequillo peppers

Crumbled blue cheese or feta cheese

Thin strips of roasted red bell peppers (see page 107)

Dab of chile paste

Thin slices of sun-dried tomatoes drained of their oil

Julienned strips of fresh basil

GARLIC CROÛTES WITH BRIE AND TOMATO-CUCUMBER-MINT TOPPING

SERVES 5 TO 10

These thin slices of crunchy French bread are grilled with olive oil and garlic. They are then topped with thin slices of creamy Brie and a refreshing, colorful summery topping—juicy cubes of tomato, cucumber, and fresh mint.

The croûtes can be made a day ahead of time and the topping can be assembled several hours before.

INGREDIENTS

THE CROÛTES

Ten ¾-inch slices French baguette

2 tablespoons olive oil

1 large clove garlic, minced

:::::

THE TOPPING

1 small seedless cucumber, peeled and cubed (about ¾ cup)

1 medium tomato, cored and cubed (about ¾ cup)

¼ cup very thinly sliced fresh mint, plus sprigs for garnish

3 tablespoons olive oil

1½ tablespoons white wine vinegar

Salt

Freshly ground black pepper

:::::

5 ounces Brie, cut into 10 thin slices

1. Preheat the broiler.

2. *Make the croûtes:* Place the slices of bread on a baking sheet and drizzle with half the oil and half the garlic. Broil for 1 minute. Gently flip the bread over and spread with the remaining oil and garlic. Broil for another minute, or until golden brown. Let cool. The croûtes can be made a day

Continued...

...*continued*

ahead of time; store in a tightly closed tin or a plastic bag and keep at room temperature.

3. *Make the topping:* In a medium bowl, gently mix together the cucumber, tomato, and sliced mint. Add the oil, vinegar, and salt and pepper to taste; check the seasoning. The topping can be made several hours ahead of time; cover and refrigerate until ready to serve.

4. Place the croûtes on a serving plate. Add a slice of Brie on top of each piece and spoon about 1 tablespoon of the tomato-cucumber-mint topping on the cheese. Serve at room temperature. Place any extra topping in the middle of the plate and garnish with the mint sprigs.

VARIATIONS:

Broil the bread for 1 minute. Gently flip it over and spread with the remaining oil and garlic and the Brie slices. Broil until *just* melted and then top with the tomato-cucumber-mint mixture.

Substitute goat cheese or another creamy cheese for the Brie.

THE CHEESE TRAY

Every good cocktail party has a cheese tray. Is it a cliché? Maybe, but do we really care? Everyone loves cheese, especially when you choose carefully and offer some surprises. Offer three to four varieties for a small party and up to six or eight for a large event. Serve them on a large wooden or marble board. Choose a variety of hard and soft cheeses, with a range of strong, full-flavored cheeses and milder ones.

Some of our favorite cheeses include Parmigiano-Reggiano (not just for grating; its sharp flavor is fabulous in small chunks); nutty Gruyère; creamy French and American goat cheese (herb-flavored, pepper-coated, and plain); sharp Cheddar; Tomme de Savoie; and a good, ripe, creamy Brie or Camembert. We love full-flavored Spanish cheeses like Manchego, Mahon, Idiazabal, and Cabrales Blue as well. Truth is, we have rarely met a cheese we didn't love. Visit a reputable cheese store where someone can help you choose a ripe variety.

Cheese should always be served at room temperature so you can fully appreciate its nuances and flavor.

Serve a good selection of cheeses with any or all of the following:

* Pita Crackers (page 73)

* Baked Pastry-Wrapped Olives (page 53)

* Orange and Chile–Spiced Olives (page 18)

* Caperberries

* Pineapple-Pepper Salsa (page 127)

* Crusty breads, breadsticks, and an assortment of crackers

* Spiced Nuts (page 33)

* Herb-flavored honey: It's especially good with blue cheese.

* Grapes, fresh figs, and slices of ripe pear, apple, quince, or melon

* Crystallized ginger cut into thin slices

* Dried fruit like dates, apricots, dried cranberries, or blueberries

* Italian *mostarda*—a jelly made with fruit, sugar, and mustard in a thick syrup

* A selection of chutneys, fig jam, and onion or garlic jam

BASIL LEAVES WITH GOAT CHEESE, TOASTED PINE NUTS, AND SUMMER TOMATOES

SERVES 10 TO 20

Kathy first developed this recipe for *Food & Wine* magazine when she had a surplus of gorgeous basil leaves in her garden. Look for organic basil— the best looking, least bruised leaves you can find.

INGREDIENTS

½ cup (2½ ounces) pine nuts

4 ounces goat cheese, at room temperature

2 tablespoons heavy cream

Salt

Freshly ground black pepper

20 unblemished fresh basil leaves, about 3 inches long

1 medium yellow or red tomato, finely chopped

1. In a small, dry skillet, toast the pine nuts over low heat, shaking the pan occasionally, until golden and fragrant, about 3 minutes; let cool.

2. In a small bowl, mix the goat cheese with the cream and season with salt and pepper.

3. Spread 1 teaspoon of the cheese mixture on each basil leaf. Sprinkle with pine nuts, pressing them into the cheese. Scatter the chopped tomato on top. Pinch each leaf together near the tip to form slightly oval bowls. The basil leaves shouldn't be made more than 1 hour ahead of time.

VARIATIONS:

Lightly drizzle the top of the cheese with a touch of Basil Oil (page 109).

Substitute toasted almonds, walnuts, or pistachios for the pine nuts.

CHEESE BALLS REDUX

SERVES 10 TO 15

Remember those cheese balls your grandmother or great-aunt used to serve at all the family get-togethers? We decided to take a look at this old-fashioned favorite and give cheese balls a new flavor, texture, and appeal.

INGREDIENTS

1½ cups (7½ ounces) walnut halves

¾ cup diced pancetta

6 ounces crumbled Gorgonzola or other creamy blue cheese, at room temperature

6 ounces cream cheese, at room temperature

¾ cup pitted dates, chopped

Flour for dusting your hands

1. Place a rack in the middle of the oven and preheat to 350 degrees F.

2. Place the walnuts on a baking sheet and bake for about 10 minutes, or until fragrant. Remove and let cool. Finely chop them by hand or in a food processor. The walnuts can be prepared a day ahead of time. Seal in a tightly closed container.

3. In a medium skillet, cook the pancetta over medium-low heat for about 8 minutes, or until crisp, stirring occasionally. Drain on paper towels. The pancetta can be prepared ahead of time.

4. In a medium bowl, use a soft spatula or a kitchen fork to blend the blue cheese and cream cheese. Add the dates and cooled pancetta and stir well to incorporate all the ingredients.

5. Place the chopped toasted walnuts in a bowl.

6. Lightly flour your hands and form ¾-inch balls with the cheese mixture. Roll each ball lightly in the walnuts, making sure to coat the balls on all sides with the nuts. Place on a serving plate. Alternately, you can assemble the entire cheese mixture into a large, long loaf shape coated with the nuts and serve with crackers. The cheese balls can be made several hours ahead of time; cover and refrigerate until ready to serve.

BAKED PASTRY-WRAPPED OLIVES

SERVES 15

We love wrapping pitted green or black olives—or better yet, a combination—in premade puff pastry. The buttery dough envelops the salty, meaty olives to create a truly addictive combination. Make these ahead of time, freeze them, and pop them in the oven directly from the freezer. Make a lot—they tend to go fast!

INGREDIENTS

2 sheets frozen puff pastry (about 1 pound), thawed if frozen, but well chilled

About 30 large pimiento-stuffed green olives or pitted green or black olives

1. Lay the pastry on a clean work surface. Using a small, sharp knife or a pizza cutter, cut fifteen 2-inch squares from each pastry sheet (30 total). Place an olive in the middle of each pastry square and gently roll the dough around it into a ball or simply fold the dough around the olive, exposing the olive through the sides. Place on an ungreased baking sheet or freeze for up to 2 months in a plastic container, making sure the pastry pieces don't touch each other.

2. Place a rack in the middle of the oven and preheat to 400 degrees F. Bake the olives for 15 to 17 minutes, turning them once halfway through baking. The pastry should be a pale golden brown on both sides. If baking the olives straight from the freezer, bake for closer to 20 minutes. Serve hot. (Warn people to let them cool for about a minute before biting into one; they are very hot.)

VARIATIONS:
You can line the pastry with various flavorings before you wrap the olive. Consider any of these possibilities:

Finely chop 3 tablespoons fresh rosemary, basil, or thyme and press into the pastry.

Press about ½ cup grated hard cheese into the pastry before you cut it into squares.

Add a very light sprinkle of grated lemon zest to the pastry.

Add a very light sprinkle of red chile flakes or cayenne pepper on top of the pastry.

SPANAKOPITA OUT OF THE BOX

MAKES 12

Spanakopita, the Greek-style spinach dish wrapped in phyllo pastry, is a classic. But we decided to rethink and simplify the dish. Here we fill mini premade phyllo pastry cups (available in the freezer section of most supermarkets) with a delicious creamy spinach mixture. The dish can be made ahead of time and popped into the oven ten minutes before serving.

INGREDIENTS

1½ tablespoons olive oil

2 cloves garlic, minced

6 ounces baby spinach

⅓ cup heavy cream

⅛ teaspoon ground nutmeg

Salt

Freshly ground black pepper

½ cup packed grated Parmesan cheese or finely crumbled feta cheese

12 mini phyllo pastry cups, thawed if frozen

1. In a large skillet, heat the oil over medium heat. Add the garlic and cook for 30 seconds, stirring. Add the spinach in handfuls and stir to cook it down, about 4 minutes. Remove from the heat and finely chop the spinach. Place it back in the skillet over medium heat. Add the cream, nutmeg, and salt and pepper to taste; cook for 4 minutes, or until the cream thickens slightly. Remove from the heat, add half the cheese, and taste for seasoning, adding more salt, pepper, or nutmeg as needed.

2. Place a rack in the middle of the oven and preheat to 325 degrees F.

3. Place the phyllo cups on a baking sheet. Just before baking, divide the spinach mixture between the cups and top each one with some of the remaining cheese. (The cups can be assembled up to 2 months ahead of time; cover tightly with foil and plastic wrap and freeze.) Bake the cups for 10 minutes (or 12 to 15 minutes if using frozen), or until the cheese is melted and the spinach mixture is hot and bubbling. Serve hot or at room temperature.

ONION AND BACON PIZZETTES

MAKES 24 PIZZETTES; SERVES 12

If you use pizza dough from the grocery store or a pizza parlor, you can put together these hot bacon-and-onion-topped pizzettes (mini pizzas) in very little time. Make the onion and bacon mixture ahead of time and pop the pizzettes in the oven about fifteen minutes before serving. They are delicious with ice-cold beer or red wine.

INGREDIENTS

8 pieces thick-sliced bacon (about 1 pound)

3 tablespoons olive oil

12 ounces onions, very thinly sliced

2 tablespoons chopped fresh rosemary, or 2 teaspoons dried and crumbled

Salt

Freshly ground black pepper

1½ pounds whole-wheat or white pizza dough, from the supermarket, pizza parlor, or homemade

Flour for rolling the dough

1 cup grated Parmesan cheese

1. Cook the bacon in a large skillet over medium-low heat for 4 to 5 minutes per side, until crisp. Drain on paper towels. Discard all but 1 teaspoon of the bacon fat.

2. Add 1 tablespoon of the oil to the skillet with the bacon fat and place over low heat. Add the onions, rosemary, and salt and pepper to taste, and stir well. Cook for 10 minutes, stirring occasionally, until the onions are soft and pale golden. Combine with the bacon in a small bowl.

3. Meanwhile, working on a well-floured surface, roll out half the dough into a square so that it's a little less than ½ inch thick. Use a 2-inch biscuit cutter or glass and cut out 12 round pizzettes. You may need to cut out 10 or 11 and then reroll the scraps of dough. Place the dough rounds on a cookie sheet, spacing them 1 inch apart. Repeat with the remaining dough. You should have 2 cookie sheets with 12 rounds on each. You can make the topping and *Continued...*

…*continued*

the rounds a day ahead to this point; cover and refrigerate until ready to bake.

4. Place a rack in the middle of the oven and preheat to 425 degrees F.

5. Using a pastry brush or the back of a small spoon, coat each of the pizzettes with some of the remaining oil. Sprinkle 1 teaspoon of the cheese on top of each round. Spoon 1 tablespoon of the onion-bacon mixture on top and sprinkle another heaping teaspoon of cheese on top of the onion-bacon mixture. Bake for 12 to 15 minutes, or until the dough has puffed up slightly, turned a pale golden brown, and the cheese and topping are melted and hot. Serve hot.

SPANISH-STYLE EMPANADAS

MAKES 12 EMPANADAS

We always figured making homemade empanadas—flaky pastry wrapped around a filling—would be incredibly time-consuming. We were wrong. This simple pastry takes only minutes to make, and while it chills you can prepare the filling. These were inspired by a recipe that appeared on Epicurious.com from *Gourmet* magazine and they can be made a day ahead of time and baked just before serving. Be forewarned: Once you start eating these empanadas, it's hard to stop!

INGREDIENTS

THE DOUGH

2¼ cups all-purpose flour, plus more for rolling the dough

1 teaspoon salt

1 stick unsalted butter (½ cup), cut into small pieces

⅓ cup ice-cold water

1 large egg, lightly beaten

1 tablespoon distilled white vinegar

: : : : :

THE FILLING

1½ tablespoons olive oil

1 large onion, finely chopped

5 ounces linguiça sausage, finely chopped (1 packed cup; see Note)

½ teaspoon dried oregano

Salt

Freshly ground black pepper

½ cup finely chopped green bell pepper

½ cup finely chopped red bell pepper

1 large or 2 small Yukon gold potatoes (about 8 ounces), peeled and finely chopped

Hot pepper sauce

: : : : :

THE GLAZE

1 large egg

1½ tablespoons water

½ teaspoon dried oregano

Salt

Freshly ground black pepper

1. *Make the dough:* In a large bowl, sift together the flour and salt. Add the butter and, using your hands, work it into the dough until the flour mixture resembles coarse cornmeal. Make a well in the center and add the water, egg, and vinegar. Mix well to make a smooth dough.

2. Place the dough on a lightly floured work surface and knead it for just a few minutes to form a flat rectangle. Wrap it in plastic and refrigerate for at least 1 hour and up to overnight.

Continued...

… *continued*

3. *Meanwhile, make the filling:* In a large skillet, heat the oil over low heat. Add the onion and cook for 10 minutes, stirring every now and then. Add the linguiça and cook for 4 minutes, stirring. Add the oregano, and salt and pepper to taste. Add the bell peppers and potato, stir well, cover, and cook for 10 to 12 minutes, stirring every few minutes, or until the potato is almost tender. Add a generous splash of hot pepper sauce. Remove from the heat and let cool. The filling can be made a day ahead of time; cover and refrigerate until ready to use.

4. Cut the dough in half and then cut each half into 6 equal pieces. You should have 12 pieces. Working on a lightly floured surface, roll out one of the pieces into a 5- to 6-inch circle. Place 2 heaping tablespoons of the filling into the center of the circle. Fold the dough in half to enclose the filling and press the edges together to seal. You may need to dab the edges with a touch of water before folding to help them adhere. Place the empanada on a baking sheet. Use a fork to make decorative tine prints into the sealed edges. Repeat with the remaining dough and filling, placing 6 empanadas on a baking sheet.

5. Preheat the oven to 400 degrees F.

6. *Make the glaze:* In a small bowl, whisk the egg with the water, oregano, and salt and pepper to taste. Using a pastry brush or the back of a spoon, lightly brush the top of each empanada with the glaze.

7. Place the baking sheets on 2 shelves and bake for 10 minutes. Reverse the baking sheets so the empanadas cook evenly and bake for another 10 minutes, or until the tops of the pastries are a pale golden brown. Let cool for a few minutes and serve hot or at room temperature.

NOTE:
Linguiça is a slightly spicy Portuguese-style sausage. You can also use chorizo or a spicy Italian sausage.

CHESTNUTS WRAPPED IN BACON

MAKES 24 CHESTNUTS; SERVES 10 TO 14

We were tempted to call this "Holidays on Horseback," because chestnuts are so associated with the holidays and we fondly remember eating "Angels on Horseback" (oysters wrapped in bacon). Here we use pre-roasted chestnuts wrapped in thick slices of smoky bacon. The entire dish takes under ten minutes to put together, and the soft, buttery, meaty chestnut mixed with the salty crunch of bacon is a winning combination. Wrap the chestnuts hours ahead of time and broil just before serving. Look for decorative toothpicks to serve these on or soak small wooden or bamboo skewers and cook several chestnuts on each stick.

INGREDIENTS

10 to 12 strips thick country-style bacon

24 roasted chestnuts (see Note)

1. Soak 24 wooden tooth-picks or skewers in cold water for about 1 hour.

2. Cut each strip of bacon into 2 or 3 pieces, depend-ing on the size (each piece needs to be big enough to completely wrap around a chestnut).

3. Wrap a piece of bacon around each chestnut. Place each wrapped chestnut on a toothpick or skewer and put it on a rack set inside a broiler pan. (Elevate the chestnuts on a rack so that the bacon fat drips down into the pan.) Cover and refrigerate until ready to cook.

4. Preheat the broiler. Place the broiler pan with the chestnuts about 6 inches from the broiler flame and broil for 3 to 4 minutes; care-fully flip the chestnuts over,

and broil for another 3 to 4 minutes, or until the bacon is cooked through. Remove and serve immediately.

NOTE:
Roasted chestnuts come in vacuum-sealed packages or tins and can be found in specialty food stores and grocery stores.

VARIATION:
Drizzle the raw bacon-wrapped chestnuts with maple syrup and broil as directed for a sweet maple glaze.

CHICKEN LIVER PÂTÉ

MAKES 2 CUPS PÂTÉ

Making pâté sounds like such a formidable task—one of those fussy French recipes that no ordinary home cook should try. Wrong! We sauté onions and good organic chicken livers, add a touch of spice, and puree the whole thing with some sweet butter and a touch of crème fraîche, and the result is a smooth, savory pâté. The pâté can be made a day or two ahead of time and is best served, in traditional French style, in a ramekin or crock surrounded by toast triangles, crusty French bread, French-style cornichon pickles, and a small crock of sharp French mustard.

INGREDIENTS

1 teaspoon olive oil

3 tablespoons plus 1 teaspoon butter, at room temperature

1 small onion, chopped

Salt

Freshly ground black pepper

12 ounces organic or high-quality fresh chicken livers

¼ teaspoon ground allspice, plus a pinch

½ cup chicken broth

1 teaspoon cognac

3 tablespoons crème fraîche or heavy cream

1. In a medium skillet, heat the oil and the 1 teaspoon butter over low heat. Add the onion, and salt and pepper to taste and cook, stirring, for about 10 minutes. Raise the heat to medium, add the livers and allspice, and cook, stirring, for 2 minutes. Add the broth and cook over low heat for 8 minutes, until the livers are no longer pink when gently cut with a small, sharp knife. Remove from the heat and drain in a sieve. Put the livers and onion in the container of a food processor and puree slightly. Add the remaining 3 tablespoons butter and the cognac and puree again. Season to taste, adding more allspice, salt, or pepper as needed. Add the crème fraîche and puree until smooth.

2. Transfer the pâté to a ramekin or crock and gently cover with plastic wrap. Refrigerate for at least 1 hour to firm up before serving.

CHICKEN SATÉ WITH GREEN CURRY–PEANUT BUTTER SAUCE

SERVES 3 TO 6

You'll probably want to double or triple this recipe—depending on the number of people you're serving—because once you start eating these spiced satés, it's difficult to stop. Marinate the chicken and make the sauce an hour ahead of time (or a day ahead of time; cover and refrigerate) and you can just grill the chicken about ten minutes before serving. If you don't have access to a grill, you can broil the chicken or use a grill pan set over high heat on the stovetop.

INGREDIENTS

1 pound boneless skinless chicken thighs, cut into ½-inch strips

2 tablespoons light brown sugar

2 tablespoons soy sauce

1 tablespoon canola oil

1 clove garlic, minced

1 teaspoon sesame oil

Freshly ground black pepper

THE GREEN CURRY–PEANUT BUTTER SAUCE

1 tablespoon canola oil

2 cloves garlic, minced

2 scallions, finely chopped (white and green parts)

2½ tablespoons unsalted chunky peanut butter

1½ tablespoons green curry paste (see Note)

1 tablespoon light brown sugar

⅓ cup cold water

1. Put the chicken strips in a large bowl or large zippered plastic bag. Add the sugar, soy sauce, canola oil, garlic, sesame oil, and pepper to taste and mix well to coat the chicken thoroughly. Cover and refrigerate for at least 1 hour and up to 24 hours. (If you are using wooden or bamboo skewers, be sure to soak them in cold water for at least 1 hour before using, to prevent burning.)

Continued...

… continued

2. *Meanwhile, make the sauce:* In a medium saucepan, heat the oil over low heat. Add the garlic and cook for 1 minute. Add the scallions and cook for 2 minutes, stirring frequently. Add the peanut butter and curry paste and stir to create a smooth sauce. Cook for 1 minute. Stir in the sugar and water and cook for about 3 minutes, until simmering. Remove from the heat; cover and refrigerate if making ahead of time.

3. Remove the chicken from the marinade and place 3 or 4 pieces on each skewer, threading them lengthwise so there is very little meat hanging off the skewer. (Or place one piece of chicken on a small skewer for small, bite-size appetizers.) Discard the remaining marinade.

4. Preheat the grill for high direct heat, about 400 degrees F. Grill the chicken skewers for 5 minutes per side, turning once, or until golden brown and cooked through. (You can remove a small piece from an end and cut into it to make sure it's cooked all the way through.) Serve hot with the Green Curry–Peanut Butter Sauce at room temperature.

NOTE:
Green curry paste is available in Asian food markets and in the specialty food section of most grocery stores.

OYSTERS ON THE HALF SHELL WITH GINGER MIGNONETTE SAUCE

SERVES 3 TO 6

There are few tastes as clean and briny as a very fresh oyster served on the half shell. We love the classic mignonette sauce—chopped shallots mixed with vinegar—but decided to take this sauce a step further. We chop shallots and fresh ginger and mix them with scallions, mirin, and white vinegar. The ginger and mirin add a deliciously fresh, unexpected flavor to the oysters. You can also try it with clams on the half shell.

INGREDIENTS

THE GINGER MIGNONETTE SAUCE

1 tablespoon minced shallot

1 tablespoon finely chopped scallion

2½ teaspoons minced peeled fresh ginger

⅓ cup white vinegar or white balsamic vinegar

1 tablespoon mirin (Japanese rice wine)

Coarsely ground black pepper

: : : : :

Kosher salt

12 very fresh local oysters

1 lemon, cut into small wedges

1. *Make the mignonette sauce:* In a small bowl, mix together the shallot, scallion, and ginger. Add the vinegar and mirin and stir well. Add a sprinkle of pepper. The sauce can be covered and refrigerated several hours ahead of time. Serve cold or at room temperature.

2. Place a bed of kosher salt on a large serving plate. Open the oysters and place them on the salt on the half shell. Place the sauce in a small bowl in the middle of the platter. Surround with the lemon wedges.

VIETNAMESE-STYLE SPRING ROLLS WITH DIPPING SAUCE

MAKES 8 ROLLS; SERVES 8

These spring rolls taste fresh and light and burst with the flavors of shrimp, rice noodles, fresh mint, and cilantro. Best of all, they can be made hours ahead of time.

INGREDIENTS

THE DIPPING SAUCE

⅓ cup Asian fish sauce (*nuoc mam*; see Note)

2 scallions, very finely chopped (white and green parts)

1½ tablespoons freshly squeezed lime juice

½ tablespoon sugar

Pinch of red chile flakes

: : : : :

THE ROLLS

24 medium shrimp, about 1 pound, peeled, deveined, and cut in half lengthwise

4 ounces dried rice-stick vermicelli noodles (see Note)

4 small Bibb or butter lettuce leaves, ribs removed, cut in half lengthwise

About ½ cup fresh mint leaves, coarsely chopped

About ½ cup fresh cilantro leaves, coarsely chopped

4 scallions, sliced lengthwise and then into 2-inch pieces (white and green parts)

8 to 10 rice paper rounds, about 8½ inches in diameter (see Note)

1. *Make the sauce:* In a small bowl, mix together the fish sauce, scallions, lime juice, sugar, and chile flakes. Taste for seasoning; it should be slightly spicy. Cover and refrigerate for at least 1 hour or overnight.

2. *Make the rolls:* Bring a medium pot of water to a boil over high heat. Add the shrimp, remove the pot from the heat, cover, and let sit for about 3 minutes. The shrimp should be pink and curled at the edges. Drain and let cool.

Continued...

... *continued*

3. Bring another pot of water to a boil. Add the rice noodles and cook for about 4 minutes, or until softened. Drain.

4. Fill a large bowl with warm (not hot) water. Line up the shrimp, noodles, lettuce, mint, cilantro, and scallions so you have all your filling ingredients ready for assembling the spring rolls.

5. Place the rice paper rounds in the bowl of warm water, one at a time, for 1 or 2 minutes, or until soft and pliable. Drain on a kitchen towel on both sides for several seconds. Place the softened rice paper on a cutting board or clean work surface. Place a piece of the lettuce in the bottom half of the circle. Place a handful (about 2 table-spoons) of the cooked noodles lengthwise on top of the lettuce. Arrange 3 to 4 shrimp pieces on top and scatter over a sprinkle of mint and cilantro. Add 1 to 2 scallion pieces on top. Fold the bottom of the circle up into the roll. Fold the sides into the middle and then, working from the bottom, tightly roll the rice paper circle up into a fat cylinder. Leave seam-side down and repeat with the remaining rice paper circles and ingredients.

6. Leave the rolls whole or cut them in half widthwise on the diagonal. Place on a large serving platter with the bowl of dipping sauce in the center.

NOTE:
Nuoc mam, rice-stick vermicelli noodles, and rice paper rounds are all available at Asian markets and in the specialty food section of your supermarket.

PITA CRACKERS

MAKES 24 CRACKERS

We love making these simple pita crackers. Cut open a pita bread—whole-wheat or white—and cut each half of the bread into triangles. Brush with olive oil and sprinkle on the flavorings of your choice. You can make the crackers a day or two ahead of time; seal in a plastic bag and keep in a cool spot. This recipe makes 24 crackers, but it can easily be doubled or tripled.

INGREDIENTS

2 whole pita breads, whole-wheat or white

About ¼ cup olive oil

Salt

Freshly ground black pepper

Flavorings, as desired (at right)

1. Place a rack in the middle of the oven and preheat to 350 degrees F.

2. Cut the pita breads open into 2 round halves. Cut each circle into 6 triangles; you should have a total of 24 triangles. Lay the triangles on 2 baking sheets with the cut sides up. Lightly brush the bread with the oil. Sprinkle with the salt and pepper and any other flavoring choice.

3. Bake the triangles for 10 minutes, or until golden brown. Remove from the oven and let cool.

FLAVORINGS

Add a pinch of the following on top of the olive oil on each cracker:

Garlic salt

Sesame or poppy seeds

Chopped fresh rosemary, thyme, chives, mint, oregano, verbena, or any of your favorite herbs

½ teaspoon ground cumin, dash of cayenne, and ½ teaspoon garam masala or curry mixed together

CHAPTER 2

SMALL
BOWLS

ROASTED WILD MUSHROOM SOUP

SERVES 4 TO 6

We like to serve this at parties in the fall and early winter. When you roast wild mushrooms (we use shiitake, porcini, and cremini), they take on an earthy, almost meaty flavor. We mix them with red onion, deglaze the roasting pan with red wine and chicken (or vegetable) broth, and whirl it up in the food processor. This soup has so much substance and flavor dimension, it's hard to believe it can be made in under an hour.

INGREDIENTS

1 ounce dried porcini mushrooms

1 medium red onion, chopped

6 ounces fresh cremini or portabella mushrooms, chopped

5 ounces fresh shiitake mushrooms, chopped

2½ tablespoons olive oil

Salt

Freshly ground black pepper

1 cup dry red wine

3 cups chicken or vegetable broth

½ cup heavy cream

Fresh sage leaves, for garnish (optional)

1. In a small bowl, pour very hot water over the dried porcini mushrooms and let soak for 10 minutes. Drain and squeeze as much of the water out of the mushrooms as possible.

2. Place a rack in the middle of the oven and preheat to 425 degrees F.

3. In a large roasting pan, mix together the onion, cremini, shiitake, and porcini mushrooms. Add the oil, and salt and pepper to taste, and mix well. Roast for 20 minutes, stirring once or twice. Remove the pan from the oven, and while it is hot, deglaze by adding the wine and stirring well.

Place the pan back in the oven and roast for 10 minutes more, stirring once. Remove from the oven and add the broth to the hot roasting pan, stirring well. Let cool for about 5 minutes.

4. Working in batches, puree the soup in a blender or food processor until smooth. Pour the soup into a medium pot and add half of the cream. Taste for seasoning and add salt and pepper as needed. Reheat until simmering and serve hot, in shot glasses or small bowls, with a drizzle of the remaining cream. Garnish with the sage leaves, if desired.

INDIAN-SPICED CAULIFLOWER SOUP WITH SPICED CASHEWS

SERVES 6 TO 10

Rich with earthy spices—cumin, turmeric, curry, and garam masala—this soup transforms plain white cauliflower. Make the soup a day ahead of time and serve hot with chopped Indian-Spiced Cashews.

INGREDIENTS

1½ tablespoons olive oil

2 medium onions, sliced

2 cloves garlic, minced

Salt

Freshly ground black pepper

1 teaspoon garam masala (see Note)

1 teaspoon hot curry powder

½ teaspoon ground turmeric

½ teaspoon ground cumin

1 large cauliflower (about 2 pounds), cored and separated into florets

6 cups vegetable or chicken broth

½ cup half-and-half or heavy cream

1 cup Indian-Spiced Cashews (page 33), coarsely chopped

About 1 cup chopped fresh cilantro

1. Heat the oil in a large soup pot over low heat. Add the onions, garlic, and salt and pepper to taste. Cook, stirring occasionally, for 15 minutes, until golden. Add the garam masala, curry powder, turmeric, and cumin and stir well. Add the cauliflower and stir well, making sure all the florets are coated in spices. Cook for 1 minute. Add the broth, raise the heat to high, and bring to a simmer. Reduce the heat to low, cover, and cook for 30 minutes, until the cauliflower is tender when tested with a small, sharp knife. Remove from the heat and let it cool slightly.

2. Working in batches, pour the soup into the container of a food processor or blender and blend until smooth. Return to the pot and add the half-and-half. Taste for seasoning and add more salt and pepper as needed.

3. Serve the soup piping hot topped with a few chopped nuts and fresh cilantro.

NOTE:
Garam masala is a blend of ground Indian spices often including cloves, cinnamon, black pepper, coriander, cumin, cardamom, and chile. It's available in the spice section of many grocery stores or specialty food shops.

LITTLENECK CLAMS IN GREEN GARLIC SAUCE

SERVES 4 TO 6

We love the intense flavors in this simple clam dish—best of all, it only takes about ten minutes to make. Serve small bowls of clams with some of the green garlic sauce poured on top and with chunks of crusty bread.

INGREDIENTS

2 pounds littleneck clams (about 20)

1 tablespoon olive oil

1 tablespoon unsalted butter

3 scallions, minced (white and green parts)

2 cloves garlic, minced

1 cup dry white wine

About ¼ teaspoon red chile flakes

Freshly ground black pepper

¾ cup finely chopped fresh parsley

1 teaspoon grated lemon zest

1. Scrub the clams clean under cold running water.

2. In a large, heavy skillet, heat the oil and butter over low heat. Add the scallions and garlic and cook, stirring, for 1 minute. Add the clams, stir to coat them well, and raise the heat to high. Add the wine, chile flakes, and pepper to taste and bring to a boil. Stir well, cover, and let cook for 4 to 6 minutes, stirring every minute or so, or until the clams *just* begin to open. Add the parsley and lemon zest and stir well. Remove the clams as they open and place them in a serving bowl so they don't overcook. Discard any clams that don't open. Pour the green sauce from the pot on top and serve hot.

PUMPKIN RAVIOLI WITH BROWN BUTTER AND SAGE

MAKES 26 TO 28 RAVIOLI; SERVES 10 TO 12

If you use premade won ton wrappers, you can put together these savory ravioli in very little time. We mix pumpkin or squash puree with caramelized shallots, fresh sage, and grated Parmesan and then accompany them with a brown butter flavored with sage. You can serve several of these ravioli in a small bowl, but when we're having a cocktail party or want a passed hors d'oeuvre, we like serving them individually in oversized Chinese soupspoons lightly drizzled with the sage butter. The ravioli need to chill for about an hour before cooking; they can be made several hours ahead of time and cooked in about three minutes.

INGREDIENTS

THE RAVIOLI

1 tablespoon olive oil

1 teaspoon unsalted butter

1 large shallot, minced

1½ tablespoons chopped fresh sage

Salt

Freshly ground black pepper

2 cups pumpkin or squash puree (see Note)

1 tablespoon balsamic vinegar

½ cup packed grated Parmesan cheese

26 to 28 won ton wrappers, at room temperature

:::::

THE BROWN BUTTER

4 tablespoons lightly salted butter

1½ tablespoons chopped fresh sage

Freshly ground black pepper

1. *Make the ravioli:* In a large skillet, heat the oil and butter over low heat. Add the shallot, sage, and salt and pepper to taste and cook, stirring, for 4 minutes. Add the pumpkin puree and cook, stirring for 2 minutes. Add the vinegar and cook, stirring, for another 2 minutes. Remove from the heat and let cool slightly; stir in the cheese.

Continued...

…*continued*

2. Place a won ton wrapper on a clean work surface. Have a small bowl of water at hand. Place 1 scant tablespoon of the pumpkin filling in the center of the wrapper and very lightly dab the outside edges of the wrapper with some water. Take two opposite corners of the wrapper and pull them toward each other, creating a basket shape. Press the dough together to create a tight seal. Pull the two remaining corners of the ravioli together, pinching them to make a tent shape. Use a dab of water to help seal up the edges tightly. Repeat with the remaining filling and won ton wrappers. Place the ravioli on a lightly sprayed or greased baking sheet in a single layer, cover, and refrigerate for 1 hour or up to 24 hours before cooking.

3. Bring a large pot or skillet with at least 2 inches of water to a boil over high heat. Gently add the ravioli, one at a time, without crowding them in the pot. Let them cook for 3 minutes. To test if they are done, remove one and cut it in half; the dough should be tender and the filling hot.

4. *Meanwhile, make the brown butter:* Heat the butter in a small saucepan over medium-low heat. Add the sage and pepper to taste and let cook for about 3 minutes, until the butter turns a golden brown.

5. Drain the ravioli with a slotted spoon. Place each one on a large serving spoon or in a small bowl and drizzle with about 1 teaspoon of the sage butter.

NOTE:
You can use a good organic canned pumpkin or squash or puree the meat from a cooked 2-pound winter squash or pumpkin.

PORK AND SHRIMP DUMPLINGS WITH CHILE-CILANTRO-SOY DIPPING SAUCE

MAKES ABOUT 50 DUMPLINGS

Making dumplings at home is a whole lot easier than you might think. If you use premade won ton wrappers, you can prepare the filling in about fifteen minutes and then assemble the dumplings and put together the dipping sauce hours ahead of time. Then all you need to do is boil some water and steam your dumplings.

INGREDIENTS

1 pound medium-large shrimp, shelled, deveined, and coarsely chopped

1 pound ground pork

¼ cup finely chopped scallions (white and green parts)

1½ tablespoons minced or grated peeled fresh ginger

1½ tablespoons finely chopped fresh cilantro or parsley

1 tablespoon soy sauce

1 tablespoon sesame oil

:::::

THE CHILE-CILANTRO-SOY DIPPING SAUCE

1 cup soy sauce or tamari

1 scallion, finely chopped (white and green parts)

2 tablespoons mirin (Japanese rice wine)

1 tablespoon finely chopped fresh cilantro

1 tablespoon sesame oil

1 tablespoon minced or grated peeled fresh ginger

½ to 1 teaspoon Chinese chile paste (see Note) or hot pepper sauce

:::::

About 50 won ton wrappers, at room temperature

Iceberg lettuce or cabbage leaves, for steaming

Continued...

...*continued*

1. In a large bowl, mix together the shrimp, pork, scallions, ginger, cilantro, soy sauce, and sesame oil. Use your hands or a soft spatula to thoroughly mix the ingredients. Cover and refrigerate the mixture while you prepare the dipping sauce or for up to 8 hours ahead of time.

2. *Make the dipping sauce:* In a medium bowl, mix together the soy sauce, scallion, mirin, cilantro, oil, ginger, and chile paste. Cover and refrigerate until the dumplings are ready or up to 8 hours ahead of time.

3. Fill a small bowl with cold water. Place a won ton wrapper on a clean work surface. Place about 1 heaping teaspoon of the filling in the center of the wrapper. Lightly wet your fingers and dab the edges of the wrapper with some water. Fold two opposite corners into the middle and press them together to seal. Lift the other two corners in to meet the middle and press together, using water to help the dough stick if necessary. Pinch all the edges to form a sealed pocket. Repeat with the remaining ingredients. Once you make 1 or 2, the dumplings will be very easy to put together.

4. Line 2 Chinese steamer baskets with lettuce leaves (this will keep the dumplings from sticking to the baskets and provide extra moisture as the dumplings steam). Place 10 dumplings in each basket on top of the lettuce leaves. If you don't have a Chinese steamer tray, place a wire rack (the kind you cool cookies on) inside the wok or on top of a large skillet and place the lettuce leaves on the rack.

5. Fill the bottom of the wok or large skillet with about 2 inches of water and bring to a boil over high heat. Stack the steamer

Continued...

...continued

baskets one on top of the other, on top of the boiling water, making sure the water isn't touching the bottom tray or rack. Cover and steam for 6 to 8 minutes. The bottom rack will be cooked first. Test by cutting a dumpling in half and making sure the pork is thoroughly cooked through. Remove the bottom rack when it is done and steam the top rack for another 1 to 2 minutes. Serve hot with the dipping sauce.

NOTE:
Chinese chile paste is a thick, bright red mixture of ground chile peppers. It is available at Asian food markets and in the specialty food section of many grocery stores.

VARIATIONS:
Substitute chopped cooked crabmeat or lobster for the shrimp.

Add ½ cup chopped water chestnuts to the filling for a good crunch.

MIDDLE EASTERN–STYLE MEATBALLS WITH SPICED YOGURT-MINT SAUCE

MAKES 30 ONE-INCH MEATBALLS; SERVES 8 TO 10

Here we mix ground beef and lamb with aromatic spices and yogurt, form small meatballs, and cook them in olive oil until crisp and golden brown. The meatballs can be made ahead of time and reheated in a 300-degree oven for about five minutes, or until warm. The Spiced Yogurt-Mint Sauce can be made a day ahead of time. The recipe can easily be doubled for a party.

INGREDIENTS

THE SPICE MIXTURE

1 tablespoon coriander seeds

1 tablespoon fennel seeds

½ tablespoon cumin seeds

: : : : :

THE SPICED YOGURT-MINT SAUCE

⅓ cup fresh mint leaves

1 cup Greek-style or whole-milk yogurt

Salt

Freshly ground black pepper

THE MEATBALLS

About 3 tablespoons olive oil

1 small onion, minced (about ½ cup)

1 clove garlic, minced

Salt

Freshly ground black pepper

12 ounces ground chuck

5 ounces ground lamb

1 generous cup dried breadcrumbs

3 tablespoons Greek-style or whole-milk yogurt

1 large egg

1. *Make the spice mixture:* In a small skillet, mix the coriander, fennel, and cumin seeds over low heat. Cook for 4 to 5 minutes, stirring occasionally, until the seeds are fragrant. Be careful not to let them burn. Remove from the heat and finely grind them in a small spice grinder or mortar and pestle. Set aside.

2. *Make the yogurt sauce:* Put the mint in the container of a food processor and pulse until chopped. Add the yogurt, about

Continued...

...continued

1 tablespoon of the spice mixture, and salt and pepper to taste. Taste for seasoning; cover and refrigerate until ready to serve. The sauce can be made 1 day ahead of time.

3. *Make the meatballs:* In a medium skillet, heat 1 tablespoon of the oil over low heat. Add the onion, garlic, and salt and pepper to taste and cook, stirring occasionally, for 5 minutes. Remove from the heat and let cool.

4. In a large bowl, mix the ground chuck, ground lamb, ⅔ cup of the breadcrumbs, the yogurt, egg, the remaining spice mixture, and salt and pepper to taste. Use your hands or a spoon to thoroughly mix all the meat and onion mixtures so everything is fully incorporated.

5. Place the remaining ⅓ cup breadcrumbs on a plate. Use about 1 heaping tablespoon of the mixture to form each meatball; they should be about 1 inch in diameter. Roll the meatballs in the breadcrumbs a few at a time, being careful to shake off any excess breadcrumbs, and place on a baking sheet. Add more breadcrumbs to the plate, if needed. You should have 30 meatballs. You can make the meatballs several hours ahead of time; cover and refrigerate.

6. Preheat the oven to 300 degrees F. In a large skillet, heat the remaining 2 tablespoons of oil over medium heat. Test to make sure the oil is hot—a fleck of breadcrumbs should sizzle right up. Cook about 10 meatballs at a time for 7 minutes, turning them from side to side, until they are golden brown on all sides and cooked through (cut one open to check—go ahead and eat it if it's cooked through with no sign of pinkness). Drain on paper towels and repeat with the remaining meatballs. You shouldn't need any excess oil, but add another tablespoon of oil if the skillet seems dry. Place the drained meatballs on a baking sheet with sides and put them in the warm oven to keep hot. Repeat with the remaining meatballs and serve hot with the yogurt sauce on the side.

CHICKPEAS AND CHORIZO

SERVES 6 TO 8

This Spanish-style appetizer combines chickpeas, spicy chorizo sausage, poblano peppers, and aromatic onions and garlic. Serve warm or hot with thin slices of crusty bread and an assortment of other tapas-style dishes.

INGREDIENTS

1 pound fresh chorizo sausage, cut into ¼-inch pieces

3½ tablespoons olive oil

1 poblano or red bell pepper, seeded and chopped

1 medium onion, very thinly sliced

2 cloves garlic, minced

1 pound canned chickpeas, drained, rinsed under cold water, and drained again

Salt

Freshly ground black pepper

Hot pepper sauce

½ cup dry red wine

1. Bring 1 cup of water to a boil in a large skillet. Add the chorizo pieces and cook for about 15 minutes, or until the water evaporates.

2. Meanwhile in a medium skillet, heat 1½ tablespoons of the oil over low heat. Add the poblano, onion, and garlic and cook, stirring for 15 minutes, or until the onion is a pale golden brown.

3. When the water has evaporated from the chorizo, add the remaining 2 tablespoons oil and cook, stirring. Add the poblano and onion mixture and cook, stirring, for 5 minutes. Add the chickpeas, salt and pepper to taste, and a dash of hot pepper sauce. Add the wine and let the mixture cook for 5 minutes, until most, but not all, of the wine has reduced and the dish is hot. Taste for seasoning and add salt, pepper, and hot pepper sauce as needed. Serve hot or warm.

CHAPTER

SMALL PLATES

POTATO AND SCALLION TORTILLA

SERVES 6 TO 8

In smoky tapas bars throughout Spain, one of the favorite dishes is a small wedge of baked eggs flavored with vegetables and potatoes, served at room temperature with glasses of red wine or sherry. They are called tortillas, but unlike Mexican tortillas they are more like frittatas than a flatbread. This tortilla combines buttery potato slices, scallions, rosemary, and thyme with fresh eggs whipped with grated Parmesan or Spanish manchego cheese. Serve warm or at room temperature.

INGREDIENTS

1½ tablespoons olive oil

3 scallions, cut into 1-inch pieces (white and green parts)

Salt

Freshly ground black pepper

1½ tablespoons chopped fresh rosemary

1½ tablespoons chopped fresh thyme

3 medium potatoes (about 14 ounces), peeled and thinly sliced

6 large eggs

⅓ cup grated Parmesan or a Spanish hard cheese, like manchego

1 tablespoon heavy cream or milk

1. Preheat the oven to 425 degrees F.

2. In a large, heavy ovenproof skillet, heat the oil over low heat. Add the scallions and salt and pepper to taste and cook for 5 minutes, stirring every now and then. Add half the rosemary and thyme and stir well. Add the potato slices and raise the heat to medium; cook, flipping the potato slices over every few minutes, for 10 minutes. The potatoes should be just tender and golden brown. Remove from the heat and, using a wide spatula, flatten the potatoes out into an even layer in the skillet.

3. In a medium bowl, whisk the eggs with the cheese, cream, the remaining rosemary and thyme, and salt and pepper to taste. Pour the egg mixture over the potatoes and place the skillet in the oven. Cook for 15 minutes, or until the eggs puff up slightly and don't look wet anymore.

Continued...

...continued

4. Remove from the oven and let sit for 5 minutes. Use a spatula or flat kitchen knife to work your way around the tortilla to loosen it from the bottom of the pan, in the same way you would loosen a cake from a pan. Place a large plate over the skillet and flip the tortilla onto the plate. Serve warm or at room temperature.

VARIATIONS:

Add a thinly sliced red or yellow bell pepper with the potatoes.

Add thin slices of precooked dried spicy sausage, such as chorizo, with the potatoes.

Decorate the top of the tortilla with edible flowers like nasturtium, chive flowers, or calendula.

PANCETTA "CUPS" WITH HERBED GOAT CHEESE AND MIXED BABY GREENS

SERVES 6 TO 12

This is one of those innovative hors d'oeuvres that gets people talking. Thin slices of pancetta—a cured, unsmoked, spiral-shaped Italian bacon—are shaped into a muffin tin and baked to form small, edible "cups." The pancetta cups are filled with an herbed goat cheese and topped with baby greens lightly tossed in oil and vinegar. The salty crunch of the pancetta blends with the creamy goat cheese and the light greens to form a fabulous first course. Best of all, the pancetta cups can be made hours ahead of time and the final dish can be assembled in minutes just before serving, making them ideal party food.

INGREDIENTS

12 slices pancetta, sliced about ⅛ inch thick (not paper thin)

4 ounces goat cheese or soft cream cheese, at room temperature

2 tablespoons heavy cream or milk

2 tablespoons chopped fresh chives or parsley

2 tablespoons chopped fresh basil, thyme, and/or rosemary, or 1 teaspoon dried

Salt

Freshly ground black pepper

1 cup baby greens, micro-greens, or mesclun mix (see Note)

2 tablespoons olive oil

1 tablespoon white wine vinegar

1. Place a rack in the middle of the oven and preheat to 375 degrees F.

2. Working with a 12-cup muffin tin or two 6-cup muffin tins, drape a slice of raw pancetta over each muffin cup. Use your fingers to very delicately push the bottom down into the muffin cup and drape the pancetta up and, if possible, over the muffin tin. The idea is to shape the pancetta around and into the form of the

Continued…

…continued

muffin cup as well as possible; it will change shape as it bakes. Repeat with the remaining pancetta. Refrigerate for at least 15 minutes and up to several hours to help the pancetta keep its shape.

3. Bake the pancetta for 15 to 18 minutes, depending on the thickness, until it is cooked through and beginning to crisp up. It should not look raw in any spots, but it should also not be burnt or overly crispy. Check the pancetta after about 8 minutes of baking; if it has flopped over or fallen into the muffin cup, you can carefully use your hands to unfold it and shape it to the muffin cup once again.

4. Remove from the oven and let the pancetta cool for a few minutes. If the pancetta has collapsed or folded over, you can try to unfurl it into a cup shape with your hands while it is still warm. Remove from the muffin cup and place on paper towels to drain. The pancetta cups can be made several hours ahead of time; keep at room temperature.

5. In a small bowl, mix together the goat cheese, cream, chives, herbs, and salt and pepper to taste with a soft spatula until smooth.

6. In another small bowl, gently toss the greens with the oil, vinegar, and salt and pepper to taste.

7. Place a pancetta cup on a plate. Gently spread 1 heaping tablespoon of the cheese mixture into the bottom of the pancetta. Top with about 1 tablespoon of the greens, pressing them lightly into the cheese. If desired, top with a small dollop more (about 1 teaspoon) of cheese. Repeat with the remaining cups and ingredients. Serve at room temperature.

NOTE:
If you can't find baby or microgreens, you may want to coarsely chop the greens so they aren't too large.

PROSCIUTTO-WRAPPED ASPARAGUS WITH LEMON AND ROASTED GARLIC AIOLI

MAKES ABOUT 20 PIECES; SERVES 8 TO 10

We like to steam fresh asparagus spears and wrap them with thin strips of prosciutto. They are served with a lemon and roasted garlic mayonnaise–based aioli sauce. The whole dish can be made hours ahead of time, making it ideal for parties. The aioli is also delicious served with lightly steamed or raw vegetables, like broccoli, cauliflower, bell peppers, fennel, and carrots.

INGREDIENTS

1 pound asparagus spears, tough ends trimmed

4 ounces thinly sliced prosciutto, cut into long, thin strips

1 to 2 teaspoons grated lemon zest

Freshly ground black pepper

Lemon and Roasted Garlic Aioli (facing page)

1. Bring 3 cups of water to a boil in a large skillet over high heat.

2. Peel the bottom 2 inches of the asparagus with a vegetable peeler. Drop the asparagus spears into the boiling water and cook for 4 to 6 minutes, depending on the thickness, or until they are *almost* tender. Drain and rinse under cold running water; drain again. Dry the asparagus spears with a clean kitchen towel.

3. Roll a thin strip of prosciutto around the middle of each asparagus spear, leaving the peeled bottom exposed. Arrange the wrapped asparagus on a large platter and sprinkle with the lemon zest and pepper. Serve with the Lemon and Roasted Garlic Aioli.

LEMON AND ROASTED GARLIC AIOLI

MAKES 1 CUP

In addition to the asparagus, serve this heady sauce with raw or lightly steamed vegetables, cooked shrimp, Pita Crackers (page 73), Roasted Garlic Bruschetta with Steak Tips (page 41), or the Lamb and Feta Sliders (page 147).

INGREDIENTS

1 head garlic, ¼ inch cut off the top to just expose the cloves

1 tablespoon olive oil

1 cup mayonnaise

2 tablespoons freshly squeezed lemon juice

2 teaspoons grated lemon zest

Salt

Freshly ground black pepper

1. Place a rack in the middle of the oven and preheat to 350 degrees F.

2. Put the garlic in a small ovenproof skillet. Drizzle the oil over the exposed garlic cloves and bake for 40 to 45 minutes, or until the garlic cloves feel tender when tested with a small, sharp knife. Remove the garlic from the oven and let cool slightly.

3. Once the garlic is cool enough to handle without burning yourself, squeeze the cloves from the skins (discard the skins) and put the roasted garlic cloves and any oil from the bottom of the skillet into the container of a food processor. Whirl for 2 seconds. Add the mayonnaise, lemon juice, lemon zest, and salt and pepper to taste and blend until almost smooth. Taste for seasoning and add more salt, pepper, or lemon zest as needed. Cover and refrigerate until ready to serve. The aioli will keep in the refrigerator for 1 to 2 days.

ROASTED BEET TOWERS WITH TOASTED WALNUTS AND ORANGE-HERB CRÈME FRAÎCHE

MAKES 8 TO 10 TOWERS

To make these impressive appetizers, we layer sliced roasted baby beets into towers with a filling of crème fraîche, toasted walnuts, and orange. The sweet citrus brings out the natural sweetness of the beets, which make a dramatic presentation for a passed appetizer or a first course. They can be made a day ahead of time and assembled an hour or so before serving.

INGREDIENTS

1 pound small red, yellow, and pink beets, no bigger than 2 to 3 inches wide (see Notes)

3 ounces walnut halves

4 ounces crème fraîche

3 tablespoons sour cream

1½ tablespoons freshly squeezed orange juice (see Notes)

1½ teaspoons grated orange zest (see Notes)

1 teaspoon dried oregano

Salt

Freshly ground black pepper

½ cup small peeled orange sections, cut into triangles (see Notes)

1. Place a rack in the middle of the oven and preheat to 425 degrees F.

2. Divide the beets and wrap them in 2 large pieces of aluminum foil. Bake for about 1 hour, until the beets feel soft in the center when tested with a small, sharp knife. Remove from the oven and let cool for about 5 minutes; peel the skins off (they should slip off easily when warm, so you can use your fingers or a small, sharp knife). The beets can be roasted and peeled a day ahead of time; cover and refrigerate until ready to serve.

3. Put the walnuts in a small, ovenproof skillet and toast them in the oven with the beets for 6 or 7 minutes, or until the nuts smell fragrant and are just beginning to turn brown. Remove from the oven and coarsely chop. The walnuts can be made a day ahead of time and covered.

4. In a medium bowl, mix together the crème fraîche and sour cream until smooth. Add 2 ounces (a little more than half) of the toasted nuts, the orange juice, orange zest, oregano, and salt and pepper to taste. *Continued...*

...*continued*

Taste for seasoning. Cover and refrigerate the mixture for at least 30 minutes and up to overnight.

5. Slice the beets about ¼ inch thick. Place a large slice of beet on a work surface. Put 1 heaping teaspoon of the filling in the middle of the beet. Add another slice of beet on top, pressing down lightly on the filling. Place another teaspoon of filling on top. Top with a small slice of beet and add a dollop of filling on top, to make a 3-layer tower. Repeat with the remaining ingredients. If you have different colored beets, be sure to add a slice of each color to each tower. Arrange the beet towers on a serving plate. Refrigerate for 30 minutes.

6. Just before serving, place an orange triangle on top of each tower and scatter the plate with the remaining walnuts and orange triangles.

NOTES:
Look for unusual varieties of beets at farmers' markets and good vegetable markets.

Use 1 orange for the zest and then cut it in half; use one half for the juice and use the other half for the orange triangle garnish.

VARIATIONS:
You can make these towers look fancier by placing the crème fraîche filling in a pastry bag with a large fitted nozzle and piping it onto the beets in a decorative pattern.

You can use a fluted cookie cutter to form the beet slices into perfect decorative rounds.

Substitute pistachios for the walnuts.

Substitute fresh tarragon, basil, or other herbs for the oregano.

Add 1 finely chopped scallion to the filling.

Garnish with tiny sprigs of basil or microgreens.

ROASTED RED PEPPERS WITH BASIL OIL, CAPERBERRIES, AND BALSAMIC

SERVES 6

A classic addition to Italian antipasti platters, roasted red peppers are sweet, simple to make, last for days, and can be used in a wide variety of ways. We roast them on a gas burner (you can also use a broiler or a grill) and present them with pureed basil and olive oils, salty capers, and balsamic vinegar. All of the elements of this dish can be made ahead of time and put together just before serving.

INGREDIENTS

3 large sweet red bell peppers

About ⅓ cup Basil Oil (recipe follows) or good olive oil

1½ to 3 tablespoons balsamic vinegar

1 cup caperberries, or ½ cup capers

1 tablespoon shredded fresh basil leaves

1. If you have a gas stovetop, heat 3 burners to high. Place the bell peppers directly on the flames and cook, turning the peppers from side to side and top to bottom, for 5 to 6 minutes, or until they are blackened and charred on all sides. You want to char the pepper skins but not cook or dry out the peppers. Alternatively, place the bell peppers on a baking sheet under the broiler for 5 to 6 minutes, following the directions above. Or place on a hot outdoor gas or charcoal grill, following the directions above.

2. Remove the peppers from the heat and put them in a brown paper bag; seal and let them steam in the bag for 5 minutes. Remove from the bag and peel, core, deseed, and cut off the inner ribs. Cut the peppers into ½-inch strips. The peppers can be made a day ahead of time; place in a tightly sealed bag and refrigerate.

3. Arrange the peppers on a serving plate and drizzle the basil oil and vinegar on top. Sprinkle the caperberries around the plate and top with the shredded fresh basil.

Continued...

... continued

VARIATIONS:

Use reduced balsamic glaze instead of regular balsamic. Simmer 2 cups balsamic vinegar in a medium saucepan over low heat for 40 minutes to 1 hour. You'll know it's done when it coats the back of a spoon and is thick and syrupy. Remove from the heat and let cool. Place in a tightly sealed jar and refrigerate. The glaze will last for several weeks. Bring to room temperature before using.

Add anchovies crisscrossed into an "X" on top of every other pepper.

Sprinkle the top of the peppers with microgreens.

BASIL OIL

MAKES ABOUT ¾ CUP

This oil is equally at home on top of grilled or sautéed fish, chicken, vegetables, beef, or pork. We love tossing it with pasta and salads, drizzling it on top of Roasted Garlic Bruschetta with Steak Tips (page 41) or Onion and Bacon Pizzettes (page 57), or serving it with a huge bowl of crudités (see page 110).

INGREDIENTS

1 packed cup very fresh basil, stemmed

¾ cup good-quality olive oil

Salt

Freshly ground black pepper

1. Combine the basil, oil, and salt and pepper to taste in the container of a food processor or blender and puree. Place a fine-mesh sieve over a bowl and pour the basil oil into the sieve. Use a soft spatula to work the basil oil through the sieve, discarding the solids.

2. Place the finished oil in a glass jar or bottle and cover. The oil will keep, refrigerated, for several days.

VARIATIONS:

Add thyme, rosemary, cilantro, lavender, verbena, or your favorite fresh herb in combination or instead of the basil.

Add a dash of red chile flakes for a slightly spicy oil.

(lined with plastic wrap) with a wide, generous assortment of vegetables. If you choose to lightly steam the vegetables, be sure to steam them for just a few minutes, then rinse under cold running water to stop the cooking and revive the natural flavor, and then drain them. The vegetables should be very fresh. Here are a few ideas:

* Radishes are attractive if you can find tiny, fresh ones that have a nice spicy bite but don't overwhelm. Trim off almost all the green but leave about ¼ inch on top for color. Leave whole or cut in half.

* Fennel is a licorice-flavored herb that is treated like a vegetable that is delicious with dips and spreads. Cut the fennel

ARTFUL CRUDITÉS

Serving raw or lightly cooked vegetables is a party classic. Instead of a bowl of boring old carrot and celery sticks, though, we like to show them off on a simple white platter or fill a big rustic-looking basket bulb into thin spears and be sure to leave some of the fennel fronds (that look like dill) on top for a great display and delicious flavor.

* Broccoli and cauliflower are delicious when they have been lightly steamed (we find them kind of harsh when raw) and separated into tiny florets. Look for purple cauliflower and arrange an assortment of green, white, and purple clustered together.

* Green beans are excellent to add to a crudités basket either raw (look for really thin ones, called *haricots verts*) or lightly steamed so they still have a slight crunch. Look for green, yellow, and purple beans (found at farmers' markets and specialty food shops) for a good assortment of flavors and colors.

* Carrots and celery sticks may be plebe-ian, but everyone loves them. Cut into thin sticks and season with good sea salt.

* Red, yellow, purple, and green bell pep-pers are delicious and crunchy. Cut into thick or thin strips.

* Endive spears are bitter greens with a naturally curved shape that provide a delicious way to scoop up dips and spreads without a cracker, spoon, or knife.

* Asparagus spears are excellent when they are lightly steamed (but still crisp); look for thin or thick spears.

* Scallions aren't often eaten raw, but some people love them, and they add a nice, tall, green element to the crudités plate or basket. Trim the ends off the scallions, slice down the green part several times, and place the scallions in ice water. The greens will curl slightly. Scallions add a spicy crunch, great with mild dips.

* Cucumbers, peeled and cut into thin spears, add great juicy crunch.

* Pea pods—snap or any kind with an edible pod—are an excellent choice, either served raw or lightly steamed.

ASPARAGUS WITH POACHED EGGS, LEMON BUTTER, AND PARMESAN SHAVINGS

SERVES 4

This is an elegant appetizer, much like a classic bistro salad that is delicious served with crusty bread.

INGREDIENTS

1 pound asparagus, trimmed and peeled (see Notes)

2 tablespoons unsalted butter

1 tablespoon freshly squeezed lemon juice

1 teaspoon grated lemon zest

Salt

Freshly ground black pepper

Tabasco or hot pepper sauce

4 large eggs

¼ cup very thin slices Parmesan cheese (see Notes)

1. Fill a large skillet with water and bring it to a boil over high heat. Add the asparagus and cook for 4 to 7 minutes, depending on the thickness of the stalks, or until *almost* tender. Drain and rinse under cold running water; drain again. The asparagus can be cooked a day ahead of time; cover and refrigerate.

2. Melt the butter in a medium skillet. Add the lemon juice, lemon zest, salt and pepper to taste, and a dash of Tabasco. Cook for 1 to 2 minutes, or until simmering. Place the asparagus in the butter mixture and warm it up over very low heat for 3 to 5 minutes.

3. Meanwhile, bring a large skillet of water to a simmer over medium heat. Gently crack the eggs, one at a time, into the simmering water, and cook for 3 minutes, until soft poached. Carefully remove each egg with a slotted spoon, letting any excess water drip off. Use a small sharp knife to trim the edges of the poached eggs into perfect little circles.

4. Place 4 small plates on a work surface. Remove the asparagus from the butter with a slotted spoon. Divide it between the plates. Top each pile of asparagus with a poached egg and spoon some of the lemon butter on

top. Scatter the Parmesan slices on top of the eggs and add a dash of salt and freshly ground pepper. Serve hot.

NOTES:
Snap or cut the tough ends off the asparagus. Use a vegetable peeler and peel off the bottom 2 inches of the stalk to reveal a paler green color.

Use a wide vegetable peeler or cheese shaver to shave very thin slices off an 8-ounce piece of Parmesan cheese.

EGGPLANT "CAVIAR" WITH TOMATO-MINT SALAD

MAKES ABOUT 3 CUPS; SERVES ABOUT 6

We love the silky texture of roasted and mashed eggplant, but we wanted to add another dimension to this underused vegetable. Here we roast the eggplant whole, peel and puree it, and then mix it with garlic, lemon juice, and yogurt. The puree is then surrounded by a very fresh-tasting salad made from red and yellow tomatoes, fresh mint, and scallions. Serve with Pita Crackers (page 73).

INGREDIENTS	
THE EGGPLANT "CAVIAR"	**THE TOMATO-MINT SALAD**
One 1-pound eggplant	8 ounces red and yellow tomatoes, finely chopped
1 clove garlic, chopped	
½ teaspoon salt	2 scallions, minced (white and green parts)
2 tablespoons olive oil	2 tablespoons olive oil
Freshly ground black pepper	2 tablespoons finely julienned fresh mint, plus leaves for garnish
½ cup plain yogurt	
1½ tablespoons freshly squeezed lemon juice	Salt
	Freshly ground black pepper

1. Place a rack in the middle of the oven and preheat to 425 degrees F.

2. *Make the "caviar":* Place the eggplant, whole, on a baking sheet and bake for 45 minutes, flipping the eggplant from side to side once or twice, until it is very soft, collapsed looking, and the skin appears wrinkled. Remove from the oven, let it cool slightly, and peel. Cut off both ends. Cut the peeled eggplant in half and put it back on the baking sheet. Use a large plate to press down on the eggplant to remove all the juices; discard the juice.

3. Place the drained eggplant in a food processor or blender and blend until almost pureed.

Continued…

... continued

4. In a medium-large bowl, crush the garlic with the salt, using the back of a spoon to create a mash. Add the oil and pepper and stir well. Add the yogurt and lemon juice and then stir in the pureed eggplant. Taste for seasoning.

5. *Make the tomato-mint salad:* In a medium bowl, mix together the tomatoes, scallions, oil, mint, and salt and pepper to taste. Taste for seasoning. The eggplant and the tomato salad can be covered and refrigerated for a day ahead of time.

6. Put the eggplant puree on a medium-large serving plate and surround the outside edges with the tomato salad. Garnish with the fresh mint leaves.

GRAVLAX WITH MUSTARD-DILL SAUCE

MAKES 1 POUND GRAVLAX; SERVES 6 TO 10

Like so many others, we always thought making gravlax at home was a complicated procedure. Turns out all you do is season a really fresh salmon fillet with fresh dill, crushed peppercorns, and coriander seeds; pour on a little rum (we know it's not traditional, but hey...); and let the salmon sit for two to three days. The gravlax is then sliced paper thin and served with thin black bread and a simple mustard-dill sauce. We love using any leftovers in scrambled eggs, omelets, and open-faced sandwiches (with sweet butter, thinly sliced radishes, and baby sprouts). Be sure to also try thin slices of gravlax on a bagel with cream cheese and capers.

The recipe can easily be doubled or even tripled to serve a large crowd.

INGREDIENTS

1 tablespoon black peppercorns

1 tablespoon coriander seeds

1½ tablespoons sea salt

1 tablespoon sugar

1 cup chopped fresh dill

1 pound *very fresh* salmon fillet

2 tablespoons clear light (not dark) rum

Thinly sliced radishes and baby micro sprouts (optional)

Crackers or thin slices black or pumpernickel bread

Mustard-Dill Sauce (recipe follows)

1. In a spice grinder or using a mortar and pestle, crush the peppercorns and coriander seeds until coarsely ground. In a small bowl, mix the crushed seeds with the salt and sugar.

2. Place half the dill in the bottom of a large nonreactive dish, preferably glass or

Continued...

...continued

Pyrex. Using a small, sharp knife, cut about 6 slashes into the skin side of the salmon. Sprinkle the skin side with half the spice mixture and place the salmon, skin-side down, on top of the dill in the dish. Pour the rum on top of the salmon. Sprinkle the flesh side of the salmon with the remaining dill and the spice mixture, patting them into the flesh well. Place plastic wrap over the salmon to cover it completely and then place a few weights on top to push down on the flesh of the fish. (We put a plate over the fish and then use 2 large soup cans on top.)

3. Refrigerate for 24 hours. Gently flip the salmon over, cover, weigh it down again, and refrigerate for another 24 hours.

4. Remove the salmon from the dish. Gently wipe off the dill and the spices. Place the salmon on a clean cutting board and, using a very long, sharp knife, cut the salmon into paper-thin slices on the diagonal. Garnish the salmon with the radishes and micro sprouts, if desired. Serve with the crackers and the mustard sauce.

MUSTARD-DILL SAUCE

MAKES ABOUT ½ CUP

Make this simple sauce just a few hours before serving it with gravlax. You can also serve it with cooked shrimp.

INGREDIENTS

3 tablespoons Dijon mustard

1½ tablespoons white wine vinegar

3 tablespoons olive or canola oil

2 tablespoons finely chopped fresh dill

1 teaspoon sugar

Pinch of salt

Coarsely ground pepper

In a small bowl, whisk together the mustard and vinegar. Whisk in the oil until smooth. Add the dill, sugar, salt, and pepper to taste.

CRAB TOSTADAS WITH AVOCADO AND LIME-CILANTRO CREAM

SERVES 4

Tostadas are like open-faced tacos—an ideal appetizer for parties or as a first course. We fry our own corn tortillas (if you live near a Latin neighborhood, you can buy premade tostada shells) and then layer them with a lime-scented crabmeat salad, thin slices of buttery avocado, and a simple lime-and-cilantro-flavored sour cream. The tostadas are easy to make, and all the elements can be prepared ahead of time so they can be assembled just before serving. This recipe only serves four, but they are a great choice for a big party, so feel free to double or triple the recipe for a crowd. You can also make mini tostadas by cutting 2-inch circles out of tortillas.

INGREDIENTS

THE TOSTADA SHELLS

1½ to 2 cups canola or vegetable oil

4 small corn tortillas (about 4½ inches wide)

: : : : :

THE CRABMEAT SALAD

1 cup (6 ounces) fresh lump crabmeat

2 scallions, very finely chopped (white and green parts)

2 large limes, 1 zested and juiced and 1 cut into wedges

1 tablespoon finely chopped fresh cilantro, plus 4 sprigs for garnish

Salt

Freshly ground black pepper

: : : : :

THE LIME-CILANTRO CREAM

½ cup sour cream

1 tablespoon finely chopped fresh cilantro

1 teaspoon grated lime zest (see Note)

1 tablespoon freshly squeezed lime juice (see Note)

Hot pepper sauce

Salt

Freshly ground black pepper

: : : : :

1 ripe avocado, cut into 12 thin slices

About ½ cup microgreens (optional)

Continued . . .

…*continued*

1. *Make the tostada shells:* In a large skillet, heat the oil over high heat. You'll need enough oil to come about ½ inch up the sides of the skillet. Test to make sure the oil is really hot—add a sprig of cilantro and the oil should immediately sizzle. Cut a small slash in the middle of each tortilla (this will keep it from curling up when you cook it). Add 1 tortilla to the hot oil and cook for 30 seconds on each side, or until the tortilla is golden brown. Drain on several layers of paper towels. Repeat with the remaining tortillas. The tostada shells can be cooked a day ahead of time. Let them cool and stack in a tightly sealed bag.

2. *Make the crabmeat salad:* In a medium bowl, gently mix together the crabmeat, scallions, lime juice, chopped cilantro, and salt and pepper to taste. The crabmeat salad can be made several hours ahead of time; cover and refrigerate until ready to serve.

3. *Make the lime-cilantro cream:* In a medium bowl, mix together the sour cream, cilantro, lime zest and juice, a dash of hot pepper sauce, and salt and pepper to taste. The cream can be made a day ahead of time; cover and refrigerate until ready to serve.

4. Place 1 tostada shell on each of 4 plates. Place 3 avocado slices on each, fanning them out so the tops hang over the shells. Place one-fourth of the crabmeat salad in the center of each shell. Spoon about 1 tablespoon of the lime-cilantro cream on top of the crabmeat. Place a lime wedge on the side of the tostadas and a cilantro sprig and the microgreens (if using) on top.

NOTE:
Use 1 lime for the zest, then cut it in half and juice it.

VARIATIONS:
Substitute 1 cup cooked shrimp or lobster, cut into bite-size pieces, for the crabmeat.

Add 1 small chopped chile pepper to the sauce to give it a spicy flavor.

Add ⅓ cup very thinly sliced radishes on top of each tostada.

LOBSTER AND GINGER-LEMONGRASS CAKES

MAKES 10 CAKES; SERVES 10

This is a great example of East meets West. We use cooked Maine lobster mixed with fresh ginger to give classic crab cakes a whole new twist. The ginger-lemongrass oil can be made up to a week ahead of time. You can also make the lobster cakes, refrigerate them overnight, and cook them to order. Or cook the lobster cakes a day before and reheat them in a 300-degree oven until hot. You will have leftover oil. Seal and refrigerate for up to one month and use in stir-fries, salad dressings, and marinades.

INGREDIENTS

THE GINGER-LEMONGRASS OIL

1 cup canola oil

1 stalk lemongrass, outer leaves discarded and inner stalk cut into ½-inch pieces

Three ½-inch pieces fresh ginger

:::::

THE LOBSTER CAKES

½ cup finely chopped onion

1 tablespoon minced or grated peeled fresh ginger

2 scallions, very finely chopped (white and green parts)

Salt

Freshly ground black pepper

1 large egg

1½ cups cooked lobster meat, cut into ½-inch pieces (from a 1½- to 2-pound lobster)

1½ teaspoons grated lime zest (see Note)

1 tablespoon freshly squeezed lime juice (see Note)

About 1 cup panko or other dried breadcrumbs

1 lime, cut into wedges

1. *Make the ginger-lemongrass oil:* In a small skillet, heat the oil, lemongrass, and ginger over low heat for 15 minutes, making sure the oil doesn't burn. Let cool. Strain the oil into a small jar, cover, and keep refrigerated for up to 1 month. Discard the ginger and lemongrass solids. Makes about 1 cup.

2. *Make the lobster cakes:* Pour 2 tablespoons of the ginger-lemongrass oil in a medium skillet over low

Continued...

…continued

heat. Add the onion and half the ginger and cook, stirring, for 5 minutes. Add the scallions, and salt and pepper to taste, and cook for another 2 minutes, until the onion is soft and very pale brown. Remove from the heat and let cool.

3. Whisk the egg in a medium bowl with a fork. Stir in the lobster meat, the remaining 1½ teaspoons ginger, the lime zest, and lime juice. Add the reserved onion-ginger mixture. Gently stir in ½ cup of the panko crumbs, or enough so that the mixture holds together. Form the mixture into 10 small cakes, about 2 inches wide.

4. Place the remaining ½ cup panko in a bowl or on a large plate and gently coat both sides of each lobster cake, pressing lightly to make sure the breadcrumbs adhere to both sides. (The lobster cakes can be placed on a baking sheet, covered, and refrigerated for up to 12 hours.)

5. Heat about 3 tablespoons of the lemongrass oil in a large skillet over medium heat. When hot, add several of the lobster cakes, being sure not to crowd the pan. Cook for 3 to 4 minutes per side, or until golden brown and cooked through. If the pan seems to be drying out,

add an additional tablespoon or two of the lemongrass oil.

6. Serve hot with a wedge of lime.

NOTE:
Use 1 lime for the zest, then cut it in half and juice it.

VARIATIONS:
Substitute crabmeat for the lobster.

SEARED SCALLOPS WITH PINEAPPLE-PEPPER SALSA

SERVES 5 TO 10

We love highlighting the natural sweetness of sea scallops by pairing them with a sweet and spicy pineapple salsa. The salsa is also delicious with sautéed or grilled shrimp, on tostadas, with chips, and with Chicken Saté (page 65) instead of, or in addition to, the peanut butter sauce. Serve one or two scallops per person on a small plate with the salsa surrounding them, or place a dollop of salsa on an oversized Asian soupspoon and top with a hot scallop.

INGREDIENTS

THE PINEAPPLE-PEPPER SALSA

2 cups chopped fresh pineapple

1 medium green bell pepper, chopped

3 scallions, finely chopped (white and green parts)

3 tablespoons olive oil

1 large lime, juiced

1½ tablespoons chopped fresh cilantro

½ to 1 small red chile pepper or jalapeño pepper, chopped, with or without seeds (see Note)

Salt

Freshly ground black pepper

THE SCALLOPS

1 pound sea scallops

About 1 cup all-purpose flour

Salt

Freshly ground black pepper

1 tablespoon unsalted butter

1 tablespoon olive oil

: : : : :

1 lime, cut into small wedges

Several sprigs fresh cilantro

Microgreens (optional)

1. *Make the salsa:* In a medium bowl, mix together the pineapple, bell pepper, scallions, oil, lime juice, cilantro, and chile. Taste for seasoning and add salt, pepper, and more chile pepper to taste, if needed. The salsa can be made 1 to 2 hours ahead of time; cover and refrigerate.

2. *Make the scallops:* Pat the scallops dry. In a medium bowl, mix together the flour with the salt and pepper to taste. Lightly dredge the

Continued...

... continued

scallops in the seasoned flour; be sure to brush off any excess flour.

3. In a large skillet, heat the butter and oil over medium-high heat. When the oil is hot (add a touch of flour and make sure it sizzles), add half the scallops in one layer, being sure not to crowd the skillet. Cook for 1½ to 2 minutes per side, depending on the size of the scallops, or until golden brown and cooked through. Repeat with the remaining scallops.

4. Place about 2 tablespoons salsa in the middle of a small salad plate. Top with 1 or 2 scallops and garnish the plate with a lime wedge and cilantro sprig. Add microgreens, if desired.

NOTE:
If you want a really spicy salsa, use the whole pepper with all the seeds. For just a little bit of heat, use half a pepper and half the seeds. For mild salsa, use the pepper but leave out the seeds entirely.

MINI MAC AND CHEESE

MAKES 30 MINI MAC AND CHEESES; SERVES 10 TO 15

We took the ultimate comfort food—macaroni and cheese—and turned it into a mini appetizer. The macaroni is mixed with grated cheese and a creamy sauce and baked in mini muffin tins. The mini mac and cheese pops out in a small muffin shape and can be served hot from the oven. This is a big hit with kids and adults alike.

You can bake the mini mac and cheeses ahead of time and then warm them in a 350-degree oven for a few minutes to reheat before serving. Don't leave them in the oven for too long or they will start to fall apart.

INGREDIENTS

8 ounces small elbow macaroni

2 tablespoons unsalted butter

2 tablespoons all-purpose flour

1 cup milk

½ cup heavy cream

1 tablespoon finely chopped fresh thyme, or 1 teaspoon dried

Salt

Freshly ground black pepper

½ cup grated sharp Cheddar cheese

½ cup grated Parmesan cheese

5 tablespoons seasoned dried breadcrumbs

Vegetable spray for the muffin pans

1. Bring a pot of lightly salted water to a boil over high heat. Add the macaroni and cook for 7 minutes, or until still slightly al dente. Drain.

2. Meanwhile, in a medium pot, melt the butter over low heat. When sizzling, add the flour and stir well to create a roux. Slowly whisk the milk and then the cream into the

Continued...

...*continued*

roux and cook it for about 5 minutes, or until the sauce is smooth and thickened. Season with the thyme and salt and pepper to taste, and cook for another minute or two, until thick enough to coat the back of a spoon. Remove from the heat and whisk in the cheeses and then the breadcrumbs.

3. Place a rack in the middle of the oven and preheat to 400 degrees F.

4. Lightly coat 30 mini muffin cups with the vegetable spray. Depending on how many pans you have, you may have to make these in batches. Place 1 heaping tablespoon of the macaroni and cheese mixture into each mini muffin cup and, using the back of a spoon, press down to condense the pasta.

5. Bake the mac and cheeses for 8 to 10 minutes, until they begin to turn golden brown. Remove from the oven and let cool for 2 minutes—you must let them cool before unmolding or they will fall apart. Place a large plate over the muffin tins and unmold them. Serve hot.

POLENTA "CUPCAKES" WITH WILD MUSHROOM RAGOUT

MAKES ABOUT 24 CAKES

Our trick for making creamy polenta (coarse cornmeal) is to use milk instead of water. We put the cooked polenta into mini muffin tins and let them sit for about ten minutes. Meanwhile, we roast wild mushrooms—chopped shiitake and cremini—with red wine and cream. We pop the polenta out of the muffin tins, sauté them in a touch of olive oil until crisp and brown, and serve them topped with the roasted mushroom ragout. Everything can be made ahead of time and assembled just before serving.

INGREDIENTS

THE POLENTA "CUPCAKES"

4 cups low-fat or regular milk

1⅓ cups instant polenta

⅓ cup packed grated Parmesan cheese

Salt

Freshly ground black pepper

Vegetable spray for the muffin pans

: : : : :

THE WILD MUSHROOM RAGOUT

9 ounces fresh cremini mushrooms, stemmed and chopped into ½-inch pieces

9 ounces fresh shiitake mushrooms, stemmed and chopped into ½-inch pieces

¼ cup olive oil

1½ tablespoons chopped fresh rosemary, or 1½ teaspoons dried and crumbled

1½ tablespoons chopped fresh thyme, or 1½ teaspoons dried

Salt

Freshly ground black pepper

¾ cup dry red wine

¾ cup heavy cream

: : : : :

2 to 3 tablespoons olive oil

½ cup grated Parmesan cheese

---

1. *Make the "cupcakes":* Bring the milk to a simmer in a large saucepan over medium heat. Add the polenta in a slow, steady stream, stirring to create a smooth mush. Cook it over very low heat for about 3 minutes, or until thickened and smooth. Remove from the heat and add the cheese and salt and pepper to taste, stirring well to combine all the ingredients.

2. Lightly coat 24 mini muffin cups with the vegetable spray (you may have to make these in batches). *Continued…*

...*continued*

Fill each muffin cup about three-fourths full, pressing down on the polenta to smooth out the top. Let sit for about 10 minutes, or cover and refrigerate overnight. If you only have 1 muffin tin, remove the polenta from the tins after 10 or 15 minutes and place on a plate; cover until ready to serve. Repeat with the remaining polenta.

3. Place a rack in the middle of the oven and preheat to 400 degrees F.

4. *Make the ragout:* In a large ovenproof skillet or roasting pan, mix together the mushrooms, oil, rosemary, thyme, and salt and pepper to taste. Roast the mushrooms for 10 minutes.

Remove from the oven, stir in the wine and cream, and roast for another 10 minutes, or until the mushrooms are tender and the wine and cream have reduced slightly. Remove from the oven. The mushrooms can be made a day ahead of time. Let cool, then cover and refrigerate.

5. After removing the polenta from the muffin pans, trim a little off the tops so that the edges look clean. Heat 2 tablespoons of the oil in a large skillet over medium-high heat. Let the oil get hot for 1 to 2 minutes. Add the polenta cakes in one layer without crowding the pan, and cook for 2 minutes on each side, or until crisp and a pale golden brown.

6. Meanwhile, reheat the ragout over medium heat until simmering.

7. Place 1 or 2 polenta "cupcakes" on a plate and sprinkle lightly with the cheese. Spoon about 1 heaping tablespoon of the mushroom ragout on top. Repeat with the remaining ingredients. Serve hot.

CARAMELIZED ONION, BACON, AND GRUYÈRE TART WITH HERBED CRUST

SERVES 8 TO 12

This French-style tart makes a great first course, with a salad, or cut into small squares and served with cocktails. We love the combination of hearty flavors—caramelized onions mixed with herbs, Gruyère cheese, and sour cream—baked inside an herb-flecked buttery pastry. We also add thick bits of bacon, but they can easily be omitted if you like. The crust and the onions can be made a day ahead of time so the tart can be put together and baked just before serving. You can also bake the tart about eight hours ahead of time, then cover and refrigerate it.

You will need a rectangular French tart pan for this tart, preferably one that is 11 inches by 8 inches with a removable bottom.

INGREDIENTS

THE HERBED CRUST	THE FILLING	
2 cups all-purpose flour	2 strips thick country-style bacon	1 tablespoon finely chopped fresh rosemary, or 1 teaspoon dried and crumbled
1 tablespoon chopped fresh thyme, or 1 teaspoon dried	1 tablespoon olive oil	Salt
1 tablespoon chopped fresh rosemary, or 1 teaspoon dried and crumbled	1 large onion, very thinly sliced	Freshly ground black pepper
Pinch of salt	1 shallot, very thinly sliced	2 large eggs
1 stick unsalted butter (½ cup), well chilled and diced	1 tablespoon finely chopped fresh thyme, or 1 teaspoon dried	2 cups sour cream or crème fraîche
		1 cup grated Gruyère or Parmesan cheese

Continued...

...continued

1. *Make the crust:* In the container of a food processor, blend the flour, herbs, and salt until finely mixed. Add the butter and pulse about 15 times, or until the mixture resembles coarse cornmeal. With the motor running, add enough cold water so that the dough *just* starts to pull away from the sides of the bowl. (Alternatively, mix the flour, herbs, and salt in a bowl. Add the butter and use your hands or a pastry blender to work the butter into the flour until the mixture resembles coarse cornmeal. Add enough water so the dough just begins to come together.) Place the dough on a large sheet of aluminum foil, seal tightly, and refrigerate for at least 1 hour, or overnight.

2. *Prepare the filling:* In a large, heavy skillet, cook the bacon over medium-low heat for 4 to 5 minutes per side, until crisp. Remove and drain on a paper towel. Crumble or cut the bacon into ½-inch pieces. Discard all but 1 tablespoon of the bacon fat.

3. Heat the skillet with the bacon fat over low heat. Add the oil, onion, shallot, thyme, rosemary, and salt and pepper to taste, and cook, stirring, for 25 to 30 minutes, or until the onion is golden brown and caramelized. Remove from the heat and let cool.

4. Meanwhile, in a large bowl, whisk the eggs. Add the sour cream and mix until well blended. Add the cheese and the bacon. Add salt and pepper to taste and the cooled onion mixture. Mix to combine.

5. Place a rack in the middle of the oven and preheat to 400 degrees F.

6. Working on a lightly floured surface, roll the dough into a rectangle about 12 inches long and 9 inches wide. Settle the dough into the tart pan, letting it hang over the edges. Gently press the dough into the tart pan and trim off the edges on the sides.

7. Place the tart pan on a baking sheet. Pour the filling into the dough and bake for about 50 minutes, or until the tart puffs up slightly and has a beautiful golden brown color. Remove from the oven and let cool for 5 to 10 minutes. Remove the tart from the pan and place on a serving platter. Cut into 12 large squares or 24 smaller ones.

MINI SWEET POTATO AND SHALLOT PANCAKES WITH TOPPINGS

MAKES 16 TWO-INCH PANCAKES; SERVES 4 TO 8

Sweet potatoes make great pancakes. They have a gorgeous orange color and they don't brown or get starchy like white potatoes. Here we grate them with shallots and give them a subtle hint of freshly grated nutmeg. We like to serve them on a platter with various toppings. Pick one or use them all.

INGREDIENTS

4 medium sweet potatoes (about 1½ pounds)

2 medium shallots, peeled

2 large eggs, whisked

¼ cup plus 1 tablespoon all-purpose flour

¼ teaspoon freshly grated nutmeg

Salt

Freshly ground black pepper

About 3 cups vegetable oil

Toppings: about 1 cup of any of the following—sour cream, applesauce, mango chutney, apple chutney

1. Using the largest holes on a cheese grater, grate the potatoes into a large bowl. Grate the shallots in the same way and mix them with the potatoes. Add the eggs, flour, nutmeg, and salt and pepper to taste and stir well to fully incorporate all the ingredients.

2. Preheat the oven to 300 degrees F.

3. In a large, heavy skillet, heat the oil over high heat. The oil should be at least 1 inch deep in the skillet.

Let it get really hot. To test, add a small piece of grated potato; the oil should sizzle right up. Use about 2 heaping tablespoons of batter to form each pancake about 2 inches wide. Add the pancakes to the hot oil, being careful not to overcrowd the skillet. Cook for 2 minutes. Reduce the heat slightly and, using a slotted spoon, gently flip the pancakes over. Cook for another 2 minutes, until they turn golden brown. To test, remove one, cut in half

Continued...

...continued
and make sure the potatoes are cooked through. Drain on paper towels. Repeat with the remaining batter. You can keep the drained pancakes warm on a baking sheet in the oven for 5 to 10 minutes.

4. Serve hot with any or all of the toppings. We like to add a dollop of sour cream to one, and then a dollop of applesauce to the next, and then the chutneys, so everyone gets a little taste of everything.

VARIATIONS:

Use carrots instead of sweet potatoes and add a pinch of ground ginger instead of nutmeg. Serve with thick Greek-style yogurt.

Add ¼ cup minced chives to the pancake batter and add very thinly sliced scallions instead of, or in addition to, shallots.

BAKED LINGUIÇA-STUFFED NEW POTATOES

MAKES 16 POTATO HALVES; SERVES 8 TO 16

These appetizers have all the appeal of baked stuffed potatoes, only in miniature. We caramelize onions and linguiça—a slightly spicy Portuguese-style sausage—and cook them until golden. We bake buttery, delicate new potatoes and carefully scoop out the flesh. We then mash the potato flesh with some milk and butter and mix it with the onions and sausage and stuff the mixture back into the potato shell. If you cut a very thin slice off the bottom of each potato half, it will sit upright on a plate and not wobble around. The potatoes can be made a day ahead of time and baked just before serving.

INGREDIENTS

8 small white or red new (baby) potatoes (about 12½ ounces)

2 tablespoons olive oil

1 small onion, finely chopped

1 linguiça sausage or fresh (not dried) chorizo sausage (about 6 ounces)

Salt

Freshly ground black pepper

1 teaspoon unsalted butter

¼ cup milk

2 scallions, very finely chopped (white and green parts)

¼ cup grated Parmesan, Monterey Jack, or sharp Cheddar cheese, or a combination

Paprika, for garnish (optional)

1. Place a rack in the middle of the oven and preheat to 350 degrees F. Put the potatoes in an ovenproof skillet or on a baking sheet and bake for 40 minutes, until tender in the center when tested with a skewer or small, sharp knife.

2. Meanwhile, heat 1 tablespoon of the oil in a large skillet over low heat. Add

Continued...

...*continued*

the onion and cook, stirring occasionally, for 10 minutes. Remove the sausage from the casing and crumble it into very small pieces. Add to the skillet with the remaining tablespoon of oil and salt and pepper to taste. Cook, stirring occasionally, for 10 minutes. Remove from the heat.

3. Remove the potatoes from the oven and let them cool slightly. Cut the potatoes in half horizontally and, using a small kitchen spoon, scoop out almost all the flesh so there is only a small amount clinging to the potato skin. Using a small, sharp knife, cut a *very* thin slice off the bottom so the potato half will sit solidly on a flat surface.

4. Melt the butter in a medium saucepan over low heat. Add the potato flesh and the milk and, using a potato masher, mash the potatoes until smooth. Add the scallions and season with salt and pepper. Mix the mashed potato mixture into the linguiça mixture and add half the cheese, making sure it is fully incorporated. Gently spoon the filling into the potato skins, mounding the filling up above the tops of the edges. Place in a shallow gratin dish or large ovenproof skillet and sprinkle the remaining cheese on top of each potato. (The potatoes can be covered and refrigerated for several hours before serving.)

5. Place a rack in the middle of the oven and preheat to 350 degrees F. Bake the potatoes for 15 to 20 minutes, or until the filling is hot and the cheese has melted. Sprinkle with paprika, if desired.

VARIATIONS:
Use a spicy pork or turkey sausage instead of the linguiça or chorizo.

Add 1 tablespoon chopped fresh rosemary, thyme, or basil to the sausage mixture.

LAMB CHOP "LOLLIPOPS" WITH SPICE RUB

SERVES 8

Ask your butcher to French-cut the lamb chops so there is a long rib without any meat, making it easy to hold the chop by the bone. The lamb bone acts like a lollipop stick. Be sure to make enough chops so everyone can have at least one.

INGREDIENTS

1 tablespoon dried rosemary

1½ teaspoons dried thyme

1½ teaspoons cumin seeds

1½ teaspoons fennel seeds

⅛ teaspoon coarsely ground black pepper

Dash of red chile flakes

Dash of sea salt

8 Frenched lamb chops

1. Put the rosemary, thyme, cumin, fennel, pepper, chile flakes, and salt in a spice grinder and coarsely grind. (Alternatively, if you don't have a spice grinder, grind them using a mortar and pestle.)

2. Pat a very light sprinkling of the spice mixture onto each side of the lamb chops, pressing it onto the meat so it adheres. Place the chops on a broiler pan or in a large ovenproof skillet. (The chops can be coated with spices, covered, and refrigerated for several hours before cooking.)

3. Preheat the broiler, placing the rack about 8 inches away from the heat. Broil the chops for 4 to 5 minutes on each side, depending on the thickness, for medium-rare meat. Remove from the oven and let cool for 1 minute. Place on a serving platter and pass with a pile of cocktail napkins.

VARIATION:
Serve with a cluster of fresh mint leaves or mint jelly.

LAMB AND FETA SLIDERS

MAKES 20 SLIDERS OR 36 MEATBALLS; SERVES 10 TO 18

Is it a meatball or a slider? Call it what you like, but enjoy the rich flavor of ground lamb mixed with caramelized onions, earthy rosemary, creamy feta cheese, and crunchy panko breadcrumbs. Make the sliders ahead of time if you're serving a crowd and simply reheat them in a 300-degree oven until hot, 5 to 10 minutes.

INGREDIENTS

3 tablespoons olive oil

1 small onion, finely chopped

1 clove garlic, minced

2½ tablespoons chopped fresh rosemary

Salt

Freshly ground black pepper

1 pound ground lamb

½ cup crumbled feta cheese

1½ cups panko or other dried breadcrumbs

1 large egg

Small pita breads, mini hamburger buns, or Pita Crackers (page 73)

Thick, chunky ketchup and/ or 1 cup Greek-style yogurt mixed with 2 tablespoons chopped fresh rosemary

1. In a medium skillet, heat 1 tablespoon of the oil over medium-low heat. Add the onion, garlic, 1 tablespoon of the rosemary, and salt and pepper to taste. Cook, stirring occasionally, for 10 minutes, until the onion is soft and a pale golden brown. Remove from the heat and let cool slightly.

2. In a large bowl, thoroughly mix the lamb with the onion mixture, the feta, ½ cup of the breadcrumbs, the remaining 1½ tablespoons rosemary, the egg, and salt and pepper to taste.

Roll the mixture into twenty 2-inch or thirty-six 1-inch meatball sliders.

3. Place the remaining breadcrumbs in a bowl. Roll each slider lightly in the breadcrumbs to coat on all sides. (The sliders can be made 1 day ahead to this point; cover and refrigerate until ready to cook.)

4. In a large skillet, heat the remaining 2 tablespoons oil over medium-high heat. When the oil is hot (test it with a touch of the *Continued...*

…continued
breadcrumbs; it should sizzle right up), add the sliders, making sure not to crowd the skillet. (You may need 2 skillets or make them in 2 batches.) Cook the sliders for about 4 minutes on each side, or until golden brown and cooked through. If the sliders start to burn or turn dark brown, reduce the heat slightly. Cut one open to make sure there is no sign of pinkness.

5. Serve hot on a mini pita with a dollop of ketchup or yogurt on top.

MENUS

Appetizers are generally served as a first course, but what about making an entire meal of nothing but appetizers? (This is our idea of heaven.) Here we present several menu ideas, arranging various appetizers into themes.

Meze Platter

Throughout the Mediterranean and Middle East—from Greece and Turkey to Macedonia, Iran, and Cyprus—mealtimes often begin with a *meze* plate. The *meze* plate is not officially considered an appetizer, but a separate part of the meal meant to bring people together with lots of little dishes and flavors—from salty to spicy—accompanied by wine, beer, or ouzo. The number of dishes served changes from country to country and event to event, but there are generally a few staples. Choose the dishes, open a few bottles of red and white wine, and you've got the makings of a unique party.

Look for a large tray or platter (copper is traditional) and top it with bowls and plates of any or all of the following:

MIDDLE EASTERN HUMMUS *(page 29)*

EGGPLANT "CAVIAR" WITH TOMATO-MINT SALAD *(page 114)*

PITA CRACKERS *(page 73)*

ASSORTMENT OF BLACK AND GREEN OLIVES

FETA CHEESE SPRINKLED WITH TOASTED WALNUTS, LEMON JUICE, OLIVE OIL, AND OREGANO

SPANAKOPITA OUT OF THE BOX *(page 54)*

MIDDLE EASTERN–STYLE MEATBALLS WITH SPICED YOGURT-MINT SAUCE *(page 89)*

TOMATO AND CUCUMBER WEDGES WITH OLIVE OIL AND VINEGAR

POMEGRANATES CUT INTO WEDGES

Antipasti Platter

The famed antipasti platters of Italy are known the world over—and for good reason. Who can resist this collection of sausages, cheeses, olives, and vegetables? Serve with Italian wines or our Bellinis (page 27). Here are some ideas for making your own antipasti:

SEVERAL HARD SALAMIS AND COOKED SAUSAGES, BOTH SWEET AND SPICY. TRY THINLY SLICED PROSCIUTTO, MORTADELLA, AND CAPOCOLLO.

A COLLECTION OF ITALIAN CHEESES, INCLUDING PARMIGIANO-REGGIANO, FONTINA, AND PROVOLONE. AND DON'T FORGET THICK SLICES OF FRESH MOZZARELLA DRIZZLED WITH GOOD ITALIAN OLIVE OIL.

ROASTED RED PEPPERS WITH BASIL OIL, CAPERBERRIES, AND BALSAMIC *(page 107)*

BAKED PASTRY-WRAPPED OLIVES *(page 53)*

WHITE BEAN CROSTINI WITH OLIVE AND SUN-DRIED TOMATO TOPPING *(page 39)*

PUMPKIN RAVIOLI WITH BROWN BUTTER AND SAGE *(page 82)*

PROSCIUTTO-WRAPPED ASPARAGUS WITH LEMON AND ROASTED GARLIC AIOLI *(page 102)*

MARINATED ARTICHOKE HEARTS AND MUSHROOMS

THIN SLICES OF CRUSTY ITALIAN BREAD

ROASTED GARLIC BRUSCHETTA WITH STEAK TIPS *(page 41)*

WEDGES OF FRESH RAW FENNEL, CUCUMBER, AND TOMATOES DRIZZLED WITH OLIVE OIL, BALSAMIC VINEGAR, AND CHOPPED FRESH BASIL

Vegetarian Happening

ORANGE AND CHILE–SPICED OLIVES
(page 18)

MIDDLE EASTERN HUMMUS *(page 29)*

PITA CRACKERS *(page 73)*

**BASIL LEAVES WITH GOAT CHEESE,
TOASTED PINE NUTS, AND SUMMER
TOMATOES** *(page 49)*

**INDIAN-SPICED CAULIFLOWER SOUP
WITH SPICED CASHEWS**
(made with vegetable stock; page 78)

POTATO AND SCALLION TORTILLA *(page 96)*

**ROASTED BEET TOWERS WITH TOASTED
WALNUTS AND ORANGE-HERB CRÈME
FRAÎCHE** *(page 105)*

Watching a Movie, the Academy Awards, or the Big Game

FIVE-ONION DIP *(page 20)*

PITA CRACKERS *(page 73)*

**POPCORN: THREE VARIATIONS
ON A THEME** *(page 30)*

**SPICED NUTS: THREE VARIATIONS
ON A THEME** *(page 33)*

**MIDDLE EASTERN–STYLE MEATBALLS WITH
SPICED YOGURT-MINT SAUCE** *(page 89)*

CHEESE BALLS REDUX *(page 50)*

BAKED PASTRY-WRAPPED OLIVES *(page 53)*

**ROASTED GARLIC BRUSCHETTA WITH
STEAK TIPS** *(page 41)*

A Quick Celebratory Drink

You're having a few people over for a glass of Champagne to celebrate something special. You are planning to go out for dinner afterward but want to serve just a few little bites:

SPICED NUTS: THREE VARIATIONS ON A THEME *(page 33)*

RED CAVIAR AND MEYER LEMON DIP *(page 22)*

CHICKEN LIVER PÂTÉ *(page 64)*

ORANGE AND CHILE–SPICED OLIVES *(page 18)*

ARTFUL CRUDITÉS *(see page 110)*

PITA CRACKERS *(page 73)*

OYSTERS ON THE HALF SHELL WITH GINGER MIGNONETTE SAUCE *(page 69)*

French Cocktails

Open several bottles of nice French red and white wine and serve any or all of these appetizers for a French theme:

CHICKEN LIVER PÂTÉ *(page 64)*

BAKED PASTRY-WRAPPED OLIVES *(page 53)* or **ORANGE AND CHILE–SPICED OLIVES** *(page 18)*

BASIL LEAVES WITH GOAT CHEESE, TOASTED PINE NUTS, AND SUMMER TOMATOES *(page 49)*

CARAMELIZED ONION, BACON, AND GRUYÈRE TART WITH HERBED CRUST *(page 135)*

CHEESE TWISTS WITH PARMESAN, ROSEMARY, AND CAYENNE *(page 35)*

CHEESE TRAY *(see page 47)* **WITH CRUSTY FRENCH BREAD**

GARLIC CROÛTES WITH BRIE AND TOMATO-CUCUMBER-MINT TOPPING *(page 45)*

CHESTNUTS WRAPPED IN BACON *(page 63)*

Asian Party

Serve beer and sake, cold and warm, and serve any or all of the following for any day or to celebrate Chinese New Year.

OYSTERS ON THE HALF SHELL WITH GINGER MIGNONETTE SAUCE *(page 69)*

INDIAN-SPICED CAULIFLOWER SOUP WITH SPICED CASHEWS *(page 78)* **SERVED IN SHOT GLASSES**

PORK AND SHRIMP DUMPLINGS WITH CHILE-CILANTRO-SOY DIPPING SAUCE *(page 85)*

ASIAN-SPICED PEANUTS *(page 34)*

CHICKEN SATÉ WITH GREEN CURRY–PEANUT BUTTER SAUCE *(page 65)*

VIETNAMESE-STYLE SPRING ROLLS WITH DIPPING SAUCE *(page 70)*

Tapas Party

Serve Spanish sherry, Spanish red and white wines, or sangria and any or all of the following dishes:

ORANGE AND CHILE–SPICED OLIVES *(page 18)*

POTATO AND SCALLION TORTILLA *(page 96)*

CHICKPEAS AND CHORIZO *(page 93)*

SPANISH-STYLE EMPANADAS *(page 59)*

ROASTED RED PEPPERS WITH BASIL OIL, CAPERBERRIES, AND BALSAMIC *(page 107)*

BAKED LINGUIÇA-STUFFED NEW POTATOES *(page 141)*

SPANISH CHEESES *(see page 47)* **AND CRUSTY BREAD**

PITA CRACKERS *(page 73)*

INDEX

TABLE OF EQUIVALENTS

The exact equivalents in the following tables have been rounded for convenience.

LIQUID/DRY MEASUREMENTS	
U.S.	METRIC
¼ teaspoon	1.25 milliliters
½ teaspoon	2.5 milliliters
1 teaspoon	5 milliliters
1 tablespoon (3 teaspoons)	15 milliliters
1 fluid ounce (2 tablespoons)	30 milliliters
¼ cup	60 milliliters
⅓ cup	80 milliliters
½ cup	120 milliliters
1 cup	240 milliliters
1 pint (2 cups)	480 milliliters
1 quart (4 cups, 32 ounces)	960 milliliters
1 gallon (4 quarts)	3.84 liters
1 ounce (by weight)	28 grams
1 pound	448 grams
2.2 pounds	1 kilogram

LENGTHS	
U.S.	METRIC
⅛ inch	3 millimeters
¼ inch	6 millimeters
½ inch	12 millimeters
1 inch	2.5 centimeters

OVEN TEMPERATURES		
FAHRENHEIT	CELSIUS	GAS
250	120	½
275	140	1
300	150	2
325	160	3
350	180	4
375	190	5
400	200	6
425	220	7
450	230	8
475	240	9
500	260	10